WILLIAM
FAULKNER

COMPREHENSIVE RESEARCH
AND STUDY GUIDE

BLOOM'S
MAJOR
NOVELISTS

**EDITED AND WITH AN
INTRODUCTION BY HAROLD BLOOM**

BLOOM'S MAJOR DRAMATISTS

Anton Chekhov
Henrik Ibsen
Arthur Miller
Eugene O'Neill
Shakespeare's Comedies
Shakespeare's Histories
Shakespeare's Romances
Shakespeare's Tragedies
George Bernard Shaw
Tennessee Williams

BLOOM'S MAJOR NOVELISTS

Jane Austen
The Brontës
Willa Cather
Charles Dickens
William Faulkner
F. Scott Fitzgerald
Nathaniel Hawthorne
Ernest Hemingway
Toni Morrison
John Steinbeck
Mark Twain
Alice Walker

BLOOM'S MAJOR SHORT STORY WRITERS

William Faulkner
F. Scott Fitzgerald
Ernest Hemingway
O. Henry
James Joyce
Herman Melville
Flannery O'Connor
Edgar Allan Poe
J. D. Salinger
John Steinbeck
Mark Twain
Eudora Welty

BLOOM'S MAJOR WORLD POETS

Geoffrey Chaucer
Emily Dickinson
John Donne
T. S. Eliot
Robert Frost
Langston Hughes
John Milton
Edgar Allan Poe
Shakespeare's Poems & Sonnets
Alfred, Lord Tennyson
Walt Whitman
William Wordsworth

BLOOM'S NOTES

The Adventures of Huckleberry Finn
Aeneid
The Age of Innocence
Animal Farm
The Autobiography of Malcolm X
The Awakening
Beloved
Beowulf
Billy Budd, Benito Cereno, & Bartleby the Scrivener
Brave New World
The Catcher in the Rye
Crime and Punishment
The Crucible

Death of a Salesman
A Farewell to Arms
Frankenstein
The Grapes of Wrath
Great Expectations
The Great Gatsby
Gulliver's Travels
Hamlet
Heart of Darkness & The Secret Sharer
Henry IV, Part One
I Know Why the Caged Bird Sings
Iliad
Inferno
Invisible Man
Jane Eyre
Julius Caesar

King Lear
Lord of the Flies
Macbeth
A Midsummer Night's Dream
Moby-Dick
Native Son
Nineteen Eighty-Four
Odyssey
Oedipus Plays
Of Mice and Men
The Old Man and the Sea
Othello
Paradise Lost
A Portrait of the Artist as a Young Man
The Portrait of a Lady

Pride and Prejudice
The Red Badge of Courage
Romeo and Juliet
The Scarlet Letter
Silas Marner
The Sound and the Fury
The Sun Also Rises
A Tale of Two Cities
Tess of the D'Urbervilles
Their Eyes Were Watching God
To Kill a Mockingbird
Uncle Tom's Cabin
Wuthering Heights

WILLIAM
FAULKNER

COMPREHENSIVE RESEARCH
AND STUDY GUIDE

BLOOM'S
MAJOR
NOVELISTS

EDITED AND WITH AN INTRODUCTION
BY HAROLD BLOOM

© 2000 by Chelsea House Publishers, a subsidiary of Haights Cross
Communications.

Introduction © 2000 by Harold Bloom

Printed and bound in the United States of America.

3 5 7 9 8 6 4 2

Library of Congress Cataloging-in-Publication Data
William Faulkner / edited and with an introduction by Harold Bloom.
    cm.—(Bloom's major novelists)
Includes bibliographical references and index.
ISBN 0-7910-5255-9
Faulkner, William, 1897-1962—Examinations Study guides.
Bloom, Harold.   II. Series.
PS3511.A86Z985685   1999
813'.52—dc21   99-25973
                              CIP

Chelsea House Publishers
1974 Sproul Road, Suite 400
Broomall, PA 19008-0914

The Chelsea House world wide web
address is www.chelseahouse.com

Contributing Editor: Aaron Tillman

Contents

User's Guide

This volume is designed to present biographical, critical, and bibliographical information on the author's best-known or most important works. Following Harold Bloom's editor's note and introduction is a detailed biography of the author, discussing major life events and important literary accomplishments. A plot summary of each novel follows, tracing significant themes, patterns, and motifs in the work.

A selection of critical extracts, derived from previously published material from leading critics, analyzes aspects of each work. The extracts consist of statements from the author, if available, early reviews of the work, and later evaluations up to the present. A bibliography of the author's writings (including a complete list of all works written, cowritten, edited, and translated), a list of additional books and articles on the author and his or her work, and an index of themes and ideas in the author's writings conclude the volume.

~

Harold Bloom is Sterling Professor of the Humanities at Yale University and Henry W. and Albert A. Berg Professor of English at the New York University Graduate School. He is the author of over 20 books and the editor of more than 30 anthologies of literary criticism.

Professor Bloom's works include *Shelley's Mythmaking* (1959), *The Visionary Company* (1961), *Blake's Apocalypse* (1963), *Yeats* (1970), *A Map of Misreading* (1975), *Kabbalah and Criticism* (1975), and *Agon: Toward a Theory of Revisionism* (1982). *The Anxiety of Influence* (1973) sets forth Professor Bloom's provocative theory of the literary relationships between the great writers and their predecessors. His most recent books include *The American Religion* (1992), *The Western Canon* (1994), *Omens of Millennium: The Gnosis of Angels, Dreams, and Resurrection* (1996), and *Shakespeare: The Invention of the Human* (1998), a finalist for the 1998 National Book Award.

Professor Bloom earned his Ph.D. from Yale University in 1955 and has served on the Yale faculty since then. He is a 1985 MacArthur Foundation Award recipient, served as the Charles Eliot Norton Professor of Poetry at Harvard University in 1987–88, and has received honorary degrees from the universities of Rome and Bologna. In 1999, Professor Bloom received the prestigious American Academy of Arts and Letters Gold Medal for Criticism.

Currently, Harold Bloom is the editor of numerous Chelsea House volumes of literary criticism, including the series BLOOM'S NOTES, BLOOM'S MAJOR SHORT STORY WRITERS, BLOOM'S MAJOR POETS, MAJOR LITERARY CHARACTERS, MODERN CRITICAL VIEWS, MODERN CRITICAL INTERPRETATIONS, and WOMEN WRITERS OF ENGLISH AND THEIR WORKS.

Editor's Note

Light in August receives distinguished traditional Critical Views from Michael Millgate and Cleanth Brooks, while feminist criticism is well represented by Judith Bryant Wittenberg.

High points of the Critical Views on *The Sound and the Fury* include Richard P. Adams, Eric J. Sundquist, and Michael Millgate.

Millgate again illuminates *Absalom, Absalom!*, as do Robert Dale Parker and Deborah Clarke.

Introduction

HAROLD BLOOM

Among all of Faulkner's novels, I have a personal preference for *As I Lay Dying* because it is his most original and disturbing work. Yet *Light in August*, *The Sound and the Fury*, and *Absalom, Absalom!* are also achievements of genius, the most characteristic narratives of the major American novelist since Henry James.

There is no one else as extraordinary as Darl Bundren, the visionary of *As I Lay Dying*, in Faulkner's world, but the three novels analyzed in this brief volume give us an extraordinary group of major characters: Lena Grove, Joe Christmas, Gail Hightower, Joanna Burden of *Light in August*; the Compson brothers, their sister Caddy, and Dilsey in *The Sound and the Fury*; Rosa Coldfield, Thomas Sutpen, Quentin Compson, and the doomed half-brothers Henry Sutpen and Charles Bon in *Absalom, Absalom!* Though these novels are Faulkner's tragedies, Lena Grove is a figure of pastoral comedy, and Dilsey is so strong that she endures beyond tragedy. Quentin Compson is Faulkner's Hamlet, and has an engaging pathos, and yet Faulkner, like Shakespeare, was primordially comic in his deepest gifts. Setting aside the preternatural Darl Bundren in *As I Lay Dying*, Faulkner's most extraordinary characters are the outrageous Snopes clan of *The Hamlet* and elsewhere: the largest American contribution to the world's humor in the Twentieth Century.

Faulkner matters most because of the fecundity of his invented world of men and of women, and yet his own voice is certainly part of his unique aesthetic value. Sometimes I convince myself that Darl Bundren is Faulkner's surrogate, and that his uncanny voice is Faulkner's own, far more than is the voice of Quentin Compson, but it is difficult to confine Faulkner to any single narrative stance. Joseph Conrad's ways of telling a story prevailed in Faulkner just as persistently as James Joyce's polyphony maintained itself, and yet Faulkner's mode finally is less Conradian or Joycean than it is Biblical. Faulkner rarely ceases in evoking, or frequently parodying, Biblical narrative. It can be difficult to sense this relationship because no man and no woman anywhere in

Faulkner can be said to bear the Blessing, not even Lena Grove of *Light in August*. Lena carries more life into a time to come, but that is hardly going to be a time without boundaries. The quest of Faulkner's people is the very different one of waiting for their doom to lift.

There is, in Faulkner's best narrative moments, a kind of ecstasy of the ordinary. That seems an odd description of the visionary of the fire and the flood in *As I Lay Dying*, or the voice that gives us the violence of Popeye in *Sanctuary*, or of Joe Christmas and Joanna Burden in their harrowing relationship in *Light in August*. Fierce action is as native to Faulkner's cosmos as it is to his ancestor Melville's in *Moby-Dick* or his disciple Cormac McCarthy's *Blood Meridian*. And yet there is also a quietism in Faulkner, a listening, as if his narrative art sought a still center, where racial and personal violence, and the agonies of copulation and dying, could never intrude. Despite the anguish that Faulkner evokes in many sensitive feminist critics, who note accurately that Faulkner's women give him no peace, doom rarely lifts in his novels unless the "female" world of love and death is evaded. ❀

Biography of William Faulkner

William Harrison Faulkner was born in New Albany, Mississippi, on September 25, 1897, to Murray and Maud Butler Falkner. The Falkner family had lived in northern Mississippi since before the Civil War. In 1902 the family moved to Oxford, Mississippi, where Faulkner spent most of his life; Oxford would later form the basis for the town of Jefferson in his Yoknapatawpha cycle. A poor student, he left high school after 10th grade, but taught himself French in order to read the Symbolist poets, and he read widely in modern English literature. During World War I he was enrolled in the Royal Flying Corps in Toronto but did not see action, and afterwards he studied for one year at the University of Mississippi.

Faulkner's first publication was a volume of poems, *The Marble Faun* (1924); apparently as a result of a printer's error a "u" was added to his surname, and the author kept the spelling in subsequent works.

After spending six months in New Orleans, Faulkner traveled to Europe; he returned upon the publication of his first novel, *Soldiers' Pay*, in 1926. The Yoknapatawpha cycle of his works began to appear in 1929 with *Sartoris* and *The Sound and the Fury*, followed in 1930 by *As I Lay Dying*. Early critical attention turned to notoriety with the sensational subject matter of *Sanctuary* (1931). Although his next two novels, *Light in August* (1932) and *Absalom, Absalom!* (1936) established him as a respected author—he was elected to the National Institute of Arts and Letters in 1938—by the early 1940s he was neglected in America and turned to Hollywood script-writing for a living.

Faulkner's second—and enduring—rise to fame began in 1946 with the publication of *The Portable Faulkner*, edited by Malcolm Cowley. He published *Intruder in the Dust* in 1948, the year he was elected to the American Academy of Arts and Letters, and his *Collected Stories* (1950) earned him a National Book Award. The same year, he was awarded the Nobel Prize for Literature for 1949; his acceptance speech in Stockholm has since become famous. Now a public figure, Faulkner traveled abroad for the U.S. State Department, visiting South America in 1954 and 1961, the Far East in 1955, and Europe in 1955 and 1957. From 1957 to 1958 he was a writer in residence at the University of Virginia. He was awarded the Pulitzer Prize twice, for *The Town* (1957) and *The Reivers* (1962), and in 1962 he received the Gold Medal for Fiction from the National Institute of Arts and Letters. Among his other works are *The Unvanquished* (1938); *Go Down, Moses* (1942); *Requiem for a Nun* (1951); and *A Fable* (1954).

William Faulkner married Estelle Oldham Franklin in 1929. They had a daughter, Alabama, who was born in 1931 and died shortly thereafter; their other daughter, Jill, was born in 1933. Faulkner died of a heart attack in Oxford, Mississippi, on July 6, 1962. ✸

Plot Summary of
Light in August

Light in August opens as Lena Grove, the most enduring character in the novel, is on the road hoping to catch up with the father of her unborn child. The man, whose name is Lucas Burch, left several months earlier, claiming that he would send for her. The reader gets an immediate glimpse of Faulkner's narrative technique in this opening scene: while action occurs in the present, Lena is caught up in reflections on the past and the circumstances that led to her involvement with Lucas Burch.

Lena is eventually picked up by a man named Armstid, who invites her to his house to stay the night with him and his wife, Martha. While there, Lena receives word that someone named Bunch is working in a planing mill in the town of Jefferson, Mississippi. Hoping that the name may have been mistaken for Burch, she makes plans to head there next. The following morning, Armstid finds a wagon driver willing to take Lena to Jefferson. The chapter ends as the driver and Lena see a house burning in the distance. Throughout the novel, Faulkner uses the burning house as a central image from which all the characters' perspectives radiate.

The narrative continues from the perspective of Byron Bunch, the man whom Lena is hoping will turn out to be Lucas Burch. Bunch recalls the occasions when Joe Christmas and another man named Joe Brown (who ultimately turns out to be Lucas Burch) began working at the planing mill. Christmas is characterized as a silent, reserved fellow who arrived at the mill wearing an old suit. His personality is balanced nicely by that of the boisterous Joe Brown, who is always found in Christmas's presence, despite the fact that the latter does not seem to care for his company. Bunch reflects on how Christmas, who worked at the mill for three years, simply quit one Saturday night. Soon after, Brown also quit; he and Christmas were thought to be involved in bootlegging liquor.

Byron Bunch himself is a resident at Mrs. Beard's boarding house. He associates almost exclusively with an ex-minister named Gail Hightower, and every Sunday he leads the choir in a country church 30 miles away. When the narrative shifts back in time to the burning house, the reader learns that this was the first time Bunch, who was alone at the planing mill that day, met Lena Grove. He falls in love with her while the rest of Jefferson's residents are watching the burning house.

Bunch tells Lena that the house belongs to a woman named Joanna Burden, who lived alone in the black section of town. He informs her that two men who had previously worked in the planing mill, Christmas and Brown, live in the one of the cabins on her property. Bunch tells Lena about the two men, describing their personalities and the rumor that they are involved in illegal whiskey trade. Suspicious, Lena asks whether Brown has a white scar beside his mouth—a scar that Lucas Burch has.

The narrative continues with a chapter on the circumstances leading to Gail Hightower's solitary life in Jefferson, his wife's infidelity, and his disgraced departure from the church. The action then resumes the day after the Burden house burns, when Bunch talks to Hightower about his encounter with Lena Grove. He fears that he gave her too much information. He also told her that he could help her locate Lucas Burch and suggests that she spend the evening at the boarding house where he lives.

Bunch introduces Lena to Mrs. Beard, the owner of the boarding house. He tells of a rumor that Joe Christmas is part black, and may have been intimately involved with Miss Burden, who was white. He also says that Joe Brown (the man he suspects is Lucas Burch) was seen drunk outside the Burden home while the house was burning. Later that night, after a $1,000 reward was posted for information about the fire, Brown appeared at the police station, claiming that Christmas murdered Miss Burden and set the house on fire.

The narrative perspective shifts again to Joe Christmas, starting with an obscure account of his experiences around the time of the murder and then shifting in later chapters to his early childhood, when he first discovered that he was of mixed ancestry. This chapter concludes as Mr. and Mrs. McEachern, an older farming couple, adopt Joe and change his name from Christmas to McEachern. The narrative chronicles Joe's passage into manhood, describing a scene when he was eight years old and McEachern placed a Presbyterian catechism in front of him and demanded that he learn it. When he fails at the task, McEachern leads Joe into the stable and belts him mercilessly with a harness strap. A few years later, Joe refuses to participate in the rape of a young girl and ultimately disrupts the gathering by striking the girl and attacking the others in the group. When he arrives home, he is whipped for fighting and for coming in late. Fed up, Joe decides to leave home for good. At 17, he escapes the farm by selling the heifer McEachern gave him for money to leave town.

Here Faulkner employs a pattern of narration that he repeats throughout the novel: after briefly mentioning a scene or event, he later returns to that place in the narrative to flesh out the details. Before Joe leaves the farm, he becomes involved with a waitress named Bobbie, who works in a restaurant/brothel where McEachern had taken him on occasion for a meal. As Joe's involvement intensifies, McEachern grows increasingly suspicious of Joe's behavior. One night, he follows the boy into a dance hall and attacks him. Joe retaliates by striking a fatal blow to McEachern with a chair. He finds his father's horse and heads home to get money from Mrs. McEachern. When he returns to town to retrieve Bobbie, he is captured and beaten by locals. After the incident, he leaves town and embarks on a 16-year journey through the South, working a number of jobs and completing a brief stint in the army before winding up at a cabin on Miss Burden's property in Jefferson.

Joe takes a job at the planing mill and becomes sexually involved with Joanna Burden, who is the daughter of an abolitionist and lives in the black section of town. She too is active in the civil rights movement. As their relationship progresses, Joe becomes increasingly unpredictable and occasionally downright hostile. The relationship acts as a corrupting force in Miss Burden's life; it alters her physical appearance, makes her less diligent with her community work, and eventually causes her mental health to deteriorate.

Around this time Joe Christmas begins selling whiskey, joining forces with Joe Brown, who moves into the cabin with him. Miss Burden tries to persuade Christmas into participating in her civil rights activities by offering to bring him on her travels and by asking him get an education and handle her accounts. Finally, she decides that his soul needs to be saved, and she tries repeatedly to get him to kneel down and pray. This persists until he meets her in her room and she reveals that she has a loaded pistol. Joe apprehends the weapon and uses it against her.

The narrative resumes as locals gather around Miss Burden's burning house. They realize that Joe Christmas and Joe Brown have been living in the cabin on her property and are now missing. After Miss Burden's nephew from New Hampshire offers a reward for the capture of the murderer, Joe Brown reappears, claiming that Joe Christmas is the killer, and also claiming that Christmas is part black. Uncertain of Joe Brown's reliability, the local officials take him into custody and bring him out on the various searches they conduct.

In another scene, Bunch and Hightower are discussing Lena Grove, who still does not know that Joe Brown is actually Lucas Burch, the man she is looking for. Bunch is in love with Lena, and he is torn between wanting to be with her and feeling that he should tell her the truth about Lucas Burch. Ultimately, he decides not to tell her about Burch, but instead makes an effort to reunite her with him. Bunch informs Lena that Lucas Burch is living in a cabin on the Burden property, where she insists on waiting for him. Bunch leads her to the cabin and pitches a tent on the grounds outside to guard her and help her if she goes into labor.

Meanwhile, Joe Christmas is captured in nearby Mottstown, after he walked into town and entered a barbershop for a haircut, not striking anyone as the black murderer that Jefferson had been hunting down. He manages to escape from custody, however, and the townspeople rally to catch the escaped felon. Later in the narrative the reader will learn that he was tracked down inside Hightower's house and shot to death.

The reader is then briefly introduced to Old Doc Hines and his wife, who turn out to be the grandparents of Joe Christmas. Doc Hines is summoned by Byron Bunch when Lena Grove goes into labor; he makes it there shortly after the baby is born. Following the birth, Byron Burch manages to trick Lucas Burch into returning to his old cabin, where he unexpectedly finds Lena and their newborn child. Lucas does not stay long before sneaking out the window and taking off again, prompting Bunch, who is helplessly devoted to Lena, to chase after him. He catches up to Burch outside of town, but when he confronts him Burch beats him. Lying on the ground, he sees Burch hopping a freight train.

Faulkner closes *Light in August* by shifting viewpoints to an "outsider" character—a carpenter who has picked up a couple with a newborn child while he was on an overnight road trip. The man is amazed and somewhat baffled by their situation: the couple, who turn out to be Lena Grove and Byron Bunch, are not married, yet the man seems hopelessly devoted to the woman and her child. The woman, on the other hand, seems unmoved by his attentions. The book ends as Lena casually expresses her delight in the places she's visited: "My, my. A body does get around," she says. "Here we aint been coming from Alabama but two months, and now it's already Tennessee." ❀

List of Characters in
Light in August

Lena Grove, the first character the reader encounters, is pregnant by a man named Lucas Burch. She sets out from Alabama to track him down, ending up in Jefferson, Mississippi.

Byron Bunch is an employee at a planing mill in Jefferson, Mississippi, where Lena arrives looking for Lucas Burch. Bunch falls in love with Lena, yet tries to help her find Burch. He learns that Burch is a former coworker at the mill who called himself Joe Brown.

Joe Christmas, the central figure in the novel, is a biracial man who becomes involved with Joanna Burden. He murders her, then sets her house on fire.

Joe Brown/Lucas Burch, the father of Lena Grove's child, establishes himself as Joe Brown upon his arrival in Jefferson, Mississippi, where he quickly befriends Joe Christmas and becomes involved in bootlegging liquor. He lives in a cabin on Joanna Burden's property with Joe Christmas.

Joanna Burden is the daughter of an abolitionist and is herself active in the civil rights movement. She lives in a large house in the black neighborhood of Jefferson. She becomes intimately involved with Joe Christmas, which leads to her insanity and murder.

Gail Hightower is an ex-minister who lives in Jefferson. His closest friend is Byron Bunch, to whom he offers advice regarding Bunch's love for Lena Grove.

Mr. and Mrs. McEachern adopt Joe Christmas as a child and raise him in a strict Presbyterian household. As a teenager, Joe Christmas kills Mr. McEachern in a dance saloon.

Bobbie is the waitress with whom Joe Christmas has his first sexual encounter.

Doc and Mrs. Hines are Joe Christmas's grandparents. They aid in the birth of Lena Grove's child. ❁

Critical Views on
Light in August

JOHN LEWIS LONGLEY JR. ON EDENIC ALLEGORY IN
LIGHT IN AUGUST

[John Lewis Longley Jr. was a professor of Humanities at the
University of Virginia. His works include *America: Society
and Civilization*. In this excerpt, Longley, Jr. speaks on the
allegorical implications of the Lena-Byron relationship.]

One need not be too far along in *Light in August* to realize that the
Lena-Byron relationship is Faulkner's Yoknapatawpha version of the
Garden of Eden, if the allegory is translated into reasonably realistic
modern terms. Byron Bunch is Adam, who labors in the garden of
the world as he knows it and is unfallen not because he is ignorant
of the existence of sin but because he is firmly established in his own
system for avoiding it. Lena is Eve—in this case, already fallen Eve,
who in a few days will give birth to the child whose father she is
attempting to locate. Byron is an Adam who will follow his Eve out
of his Garden, even though she does not particularly ask him to
follow her. The Eden that he has created for himself is austere and
spiritual but not unreasonably severe or unpleasant. Without
laboring the comparison, we could assert that the graph of Byron's
effort at heroism (though comic) traces the Christian paradox of the
Fortunate Fall: Byron will leave his cloistered Eden to plunge into
the active life—to know sin and run the risk of damnation in order
to be the protector of Lena and her child. He is well aware of the
ridiculousness of his position and of the sin inherent in his love for
Lena, but he continues to suffer that humiliation in his determina-
tion to help the two of them. Faulkner presents Byron's quixotic
adventures with a mixture of love and irony but, unhappily for the
reader, ends the story just when he is about to begin his picaresque
journey with Lena and the baby.

In describing Byron as a man who carefully avoids temptation and
idleness, it is essential to make clear that he is by no means a prig or
a prude, even in the early stages of the book. It is simply that he does
not let himself take up the usual forms of dissipation common to
young men in his time and place. He is well liked by his fellow

workers, who respect and are impressed by his austere way of life even though they would not adopt it for themselves. He displays some ability at ratiocination in his theological discussions with Hightower, but as he will discover ruefully later on, he can never become a very skillful liar. He shows some imagination and even wit in his comments on "Brown" (as Lucas Burch calls himself), when "Brown" first comes to the planing mill to work. As the rest of the novel demonstrates, Lucas Bunch is very nearly the epitome of loud-mouthed, half-witted worthlessness. Byron says, "'He puts me in mind of one of these cars running along the street with a radio in it. You can't make out what it is saying and the car aint going anywhere in particular and when you look at it close you see that there aint even anybody in it.'"

—John Lewis Longley Jr., *The Tragic Mask: A Study of Faulkner's Heroes* (Chapel Hill: University of North Carolina Press, 1957): pp. 51–52

(ᘐ)

MICHAEL MILLGATE ON JOE CHRISTMAS AS A SACRIFICIAL VICTIM

[Michael Millgate is a professor of English at the University of Toronto, where he has taught since 1967. He has authored or edited more than 20 books, including *William Faulkner* and *Lion in the Garden: Interviews with William Faulkner, 1926–1962*. In this excerpt, Millgate speaks of Joe Christmas' attempts to break free from his destiny.]

Ironically, the supreme act of violence by which Christmas frees himself from Miss Burden is the direct cause of his becoming finally categorised by society as a "nigger murderer," to be hunted down and disposed of according to the established rituals by which Southern society disposes of all "nigger murderers." Christmas's attempts to break free of his destiny are perpetually frustrated, and he is frequently associated in the novel with images of the circle, most explicitly at the end of Ch. 14, when he is travelling in the Negro waggon to Mottstown to give himself up:

Looking, he can see the smoke low on the sky, beyond an imperceptible corner; he is entering it again, the street which ran for thirty years. It had been a paved street, where going should be fast. It had made a circle and he is still inside of it. Though during the last seven days he has had no paved street, yet he has travelled further than in all the thirty years before. And yet he is still inside the circle. "And yet I have been further in these seven days than in all the thirty years," he thinks. "But I have never got outside that circle. I have never broken out of the ring of what I have already done and cannot ever undo", he thinks quietly, sitting on the seat, the black shoes smelling of negro: that mark on his ankles the gauge definite and ineradicable of the black tide creeping up his legs, moving from his feet upward as death moves.

Christmas wants only rest and quiet—a little earlier, feeling the freshness of the dawn, he realises with amazement: "'That was all I wanted. . . . That didn't seem a whole lot to ask in thirty years'"—but peace is the one thing that his past and his environment will not permit him. He must run always in his terrible circle, not in any sense a villain, as Faulkner is at pains to emphasise, but a man doomed, the victim of his heredity and upbringing and of society at large. The main function of the much-discussed Christ-imagery which clusters around Christmas, especially at the moment of his death, is not to make him a "Christ-figure"—an unnecessarily portentous term—but to underline his role as a sacrificial victim.

Christmas, after all, is not the bearer of the positive values of the novel, but the tragic helpless victim of "naturalistic" fiction, destroyed by forces beyond his control. The sense of resurgent hope, of endurance, of new life which emerges at the end of the novel is mainly embodied in the figure of Lena Grove. Not only does Lena both begin and end the novel, as if to frame and contain the story of Christmas, but her steady imperturbable onward linear progress through the book is in direct contrast to the other's frantic circling. Like Eula Varner of *The Hamlet,* Lena, healthy, handsome, fertile, rather stupid, is one of those "earth-mother" figures of Faulkner's who are perhaps nearer to his Negroes than to any other of his white women.

—Michael Millgate, *William Faulkner* (New York: Grove Press, 1961): pp. 46–48

PETER SWIGGART ON RELIGION AND RACIAL VIOLENCE IN *LIGHT IN AUGUST*

[Peter Swiggart is a Faulkner scholar and the recipient of a grant from the University Research Institute of the University of Texas. He is the author of the book *The Art of Faulkner's Novels*. In this excerpt, Swiggart discusses the relationship between race and religion in *Light in August*.]

In the narrative world of *Light in August* emotion itself seems to adopt the posture and pose of impersonal rapture and martyrdom. Hearing the sound of church singing, the Reverend Hightower describes the Southern mind and heart as being "expiated by the stern and formal fury" of its Sunday morning service. Whereas the voices of the singers adopt "the shapes and attitudes of crucifixions, ecstatic, solemn, and profound," the music itself is "stern and implacable, deliberate and without passion." That is to say, puritans tend to express their emotions, if at all, within the framework of rigid social conventions.

Puritan emotion occasionally breaks out in unrestrained violence, as in the mass fury of a lynching mob, but such violence is not a spontaneous expression of pent-up emotions. According to Faulkner the puritan mind avoids natural expression of feelings. "Pleasure, ecstasy, they cannot seem to bear: their escape from it is in violence, in drinking and fighting and praying." By forcing human emotions into the service of abstract convictions, these Southerners transform themselves into moral fanatics. Hightower explains that a mob of Southern churchgoers will lynch Joe Christmas in order to stifle their own consciences. They will crucify him gladly, "since to pity him would be to admit selfdoubt and to hope for and need pity themselves." In other words the whole town will resort to a stylized and traditional act of violence rather than admit emotional realities.

This combination of moral conviction and ruthless violence is succinctly characterized by the desire of Calvin Burden, Joanna Burden's grandfather, to "beat the loving God" into his four children. This staunch figure stands for a tradition of New England Puritanism that is related in both spirit and doctrinal roots to the more evangelical Presbyterian sects dominating the American Middle West and Deep South. It is significant that he reads the Bible to his children in Spanish, a language which they cannot understand. What they do understand is a series of impromptu sermons, composed half of "bleak and bloodless" New England logic and "half of immediate hellfire and tangible brimstone of which any country Methodist circuit rider would have been proud." The result is the Protestant blend of emotionalism and abstract morality which Faulkner consistently satirizes.

Faulkner's aim in introducing Calvin Burden and his New England heritage is to show the relation between the attitude of the abolitionist Burdens toward the Southern Negro and the racial hatred of a man like Doc Hines. Whereas Hines sees his grandson's Negro ancestry as a token of the Devil, the Burdens look upon Negroes as the sign and symbol of the white man's moral sin. Joanna Burden sees the curse of slavery as a "black shadow in the shape of a cross" falling upon all white children. The curse of the black race is the irrevocable fate of being held in bondage, "but the curse of the white race is the black man who will be forever God's chosen own because He once cursed him." The Burdens take up social work among the Negroes in the postwar South as a step toward expiating the curse which has fallen upon their own white blood. Their abstract approach to the race problem is comparable to that of Hines, who reacts in hatred to his similar belief that the Negro race is a curse upon the white. Joe Christmas inherits the prejudice of his grandfather, but he is also influenced by Joanna Burden and presumably by the doctrines which her family represents. Faulkner's references to the religious heritages of both New England and the South link social and political issues involving all of America to the racial obsession underlying Joe's violence.

—Peter Swiggart, The Art of Faulkner's Novels (Austin: University of Texas Press, 1962): pp. 133–34

☙

François Pitavy on Faulkner's Use of Light and Color

[François Pitavy is a professor of American Studies at the University of Dijon, France. He has published numerous articles in American and French journals and is the author of *Faulkner's* Light in August. In this excerpt, Pitavy observes Faulkner's use of light and color in his novels.]

Light, or its absence, is even more important than immobility in defining the landscape of *Light in August*. Hence the relative rarity of color touches only makes their effect more striking. They do not describe an actual scene so much as they express a personal vision. Yellow is the color of sunrise ("the gray and yellow of dawn") before the harsh, implacable glare of noon has obliterated every nuance of color. There is often a hint of precosity in Faulkner's descriptions of the tints of dawn: the rising sun may be "primrose" or "jonquilcolored"): Faulkner's apparent predilection for this color leads him to use it again and again, for instance, in *The Wild Palms* and *The Hamlet*. As daylight fades, the yellow returns with ominous undertones: it turns copper, as on the evening when Addie Bundren "lays dying," or when Hightower makes his confession: "that fading copper light would seem almost audible, like a dying yellow fall of trumpets. . . ." At dusk, the light takes on a purple hue and is again expressed through studiedly refined floral equivalents (perhaps a trace of Faulkner's acquaintance with symbolist and "decadent" poetry): "Then the copper faded into lilac, into the fading lilac of full dusk." Later on, in the fantastic stillness of dusk, before everything is submerged in darkness, the light is a glaucous green shade: "the world hangs in a green suspension in color and texture like light through colored glass."

These examples show that the rare and studied colors of Faulkner's world are designed less to describe a given landscape than to render impressions and feelings. Copper is the color of the other world evoked by the dying light of day. Purple is tragic, and appropriately the color of Mrs. Hines's gown, less in description than in suggestion of her tragic being; so much so that Faulkner eventually uses "regal and moribund" instead of purple, substituting the connotations of the color for the color itself, creating it anew from within.

—François Pitavy, *Faulkner's Light in August* (Bloomington, IN: Indiana University Press, 1973): pp. 87–88

Alan Warren Friedman on Character Identity in *Light in August*

[Alan Warren Friedman is the former Senior Fulbright Professor at the University of Lancaster, England, and is currently a professor of English at the University of Texas at Austin. He has published numerous articles and books on English and literary studies, including a book entitled *William Faulkner*. In this excerpt, Friedman observes the characters' quest for identity in *Light in August*.]

Light in August is unique among Faulkner's novels not in its obsessive, reiterated failures but in the framing context in which its gothic horrors occur: kindliness, serenity, motion that is linear and progressive, natural fecundity. The novel begins and ends with Lena Grove—first pregnant then, lighter in August, a mother—as she journeys, aided only by the instinctive generosity of strangers, from Alabama to Mississippi (where the novel's action occurs) and then to Tennessee. Tracking Lucas Burch, her baby's father, she seems almost indifferent to his fleeing from her when they finally meet in the novel as he had after impregnating her. Her serenity, in fact, is threatened only when, right after the birth, it seems that she might actually reclaim Lucas and lose Byron Bunch, the novel's quixotic hero who, on sight, falls hopelessly in love with her. By the end, Lucas has come to seem far more traveling's excuse than its goal, the putative quest for respectability allowing Lena—as the amused furniture dealer who narrates the last chapter in bed to his wife expresses it—"to travel a little further and see as much as she could, since I reckon she knew that when she settled down this time, it would likely be for the rest of her life."

Settling down, domesticity, is exactly what fails all of the other major characters in the novel, and vice versa; burdened with inherited visions of disaster and doom, they are incapable of defining viable roles for themselves as spouses, parents, or children. They remain outsiders, strangers, wherever they live, and consequently destroy those closest to them and themselves. Lacking the immediacy of parental influence, Joe Christmas, Joanna Burden, and the Reverend Gail Hightower are all literally or figuratively haunted by monomaniacal grandfathers who seem bent on denying them the unique origins and individuality common to the rest of humankind.

Faulkner has said that he began the novel with the placid image of Lena en route to give birth but that Christmas, most obsessed of all his characters with his origins and most ignorant of them, defines "the tragic, central idea of the story—that he didn't know what he was, and there was no way possible in life for him to find out. Which to me is the most tragic condition a man could find himself in—not to know what he is and to know that he will never know." His grandfather Hines, we learn late in the novel, had killed his daughter's lover because he was convinced he had black blood; he then refused his daughter a doctor, and so caused her to die in childbirth. Left on the doorstep of an orphanage on Christmas eve, the baby received the name that marks him as an alien, a pariah, all his life:

> "Is he a foreigner?"
> "Did you ever hear of a white man named Christmas?" the foreman said.
> "I never heard of nobody a-tall named it," the other said.

Joe's years in the orphanage are literally watched over "with a profound and unflagging attention" by the "mad eyes" of Hines whose presence, as janitor, thus sets Joe apart from the other children, who ridicule him with the taunt of "nigger." Adopted at the age of five by the Calvinist Simon McEachern, Joe moves from one religious fanaticism to another. Enduring a harsh upbringing (he is beaten when he fails, or refuses, to learn the catechism), he acquires neither self-understanding nor knowledge of how to survive in a world of ambivalent demands and offers, but only the self-stigmatizing label "nigger" that he claims for himself at the most inconvenient times. When actually asked directly, however, he acknowledges ignorance, and then wryly adds, "If I'm not, damned if I ⟨haven't wasted⟩ a lot of time."

—Alan Warren Friedman, *William Faulkner* (New York: Ungar Publishing, 1984): pp. 88–90

⊗

Cleanth Brooks on Lena Grove's Symbolism

[Cleanth Brooks was the Gray Professor Emeritus of Rhetoric at Yale University. He is the author of more than

20 books, including *William Faulkner: The Yoknapatawpha Country*. In this excerpt, Brooks discusses Lena Grove as an earth goddess.]

⟨*Light in August* contains one of⟩ Faulkner's so-called earth goddesses, Lena Grove. . . . The term *earth goddess*, however, is not wholly accurate. True, ⟨she⟩ embod⟨ies⟩ to an intense degree the vitality of nature. Lena can fairly be called an earth goddess, for she is truly of the earth, earthy. Although she is not grubby or coarse, she does respond, apparently effortlessly, to the natural rhythms of growth and development to which the earth itself responds. If in a sense she is the force that harbors the seed and brings the germinating organism to perfection, if she is the sexual force renewing and sustaining the animate world, she is not at all the sexual temptress using lures and wiles.

There is not the slightest hint that she ever strove to attract the wretched weakling who got her with child, or that later on she makes the slightest effort to capture the love of Byron Bunch. It is more a matter of her simply trusting her natural instincts to carry her to a complete sexual fulfillment in the birth of her child. Her charm is her complete freedom from guile or calculation. She resembles "the lilies of the field, . . . they toil not, neither do they spin," or, we could say, she is like "the fowls of the air [which] sow not, neither do they reap, nor gather into barns." It is Lena's simplicity and her boundless faith that all will finally be well that carry her through.

Faulkner does not, of course, make the mistake of trying to pass her off as either a saint or a charmingly instinctive animal. He provides the little touches that render her human and feminine—as when, eating sardines, she congratulates herself that she eats like a lady; or her moments of coquetry with her ardent but tongue-tied lover, Byron Bunch.

Bunch had at first sight fallen in love with this obviously pregnant girl and had, like the perfect knight, cared for her and protected her through her lying-in and the birth of her child. At the end of the novel he is still accompanying her on a wild-goose chase after the child's father, who obviously has no intention of marrying her and has fled the country.

After some three weeks of travel, Byron is sore beset. Lena seems to have no intention of giving up the fruitless pursuit of her seducer and marrying her true lover, who has manifested his utter devotion to her in every way. At last Byron tears himself away from Lena, but next day rushes back in time to rejoin her as she prepares to go on. Byron mutters by way of explanation: "I done come too far now. I be dog if I'm going to quit now."

To which Lena coolly replies: "Aint nobody never said for you to quit." This is as much encouragement as she doles out to her unhappy lover, and this is what I mean by her coquetry. But as we lay down the novel, we realize that her drop of encouragement will be enough—that Lena will eventually give up her absurd search, marry her faithful lover, and settle down.

If Lena is of the earth, almost as "natural" as nature itself, Faulkner's other earth goddess, Eula Varner ⟨in *The Hamlet*⟩, is hardly of this earth at all. She is depicted almost as a fertility goddess. She is intensely female and casts a spell over any man who views her. Here is Faulkner's initial description of her:

> She was the last of the sixteen children, the baby, though she had overtaken and passed her mother in height in her tenth year. Now, though not yet thirteen years old, she was already bigger than most grown women and even her breasts were no longer the little, hard, fiercely-pointed cones of puberty or even maidenhood. On the contrary, her entire appearance suggested some symbology out of the old Dionysi[a]c times—honey in sunlight and bursting grapes, the writhen bleeding of the crushed fecundated vine beneath the hard rapacious trampling goat-hoof. She seemed to be not a living integer of her contemporary scene, but rather to exist in a teeming vacuum in which her days followed one another as though behind sound-proof glass, where she seemed to listen in sullen bemusement, with a weary wisdom heired of all mammalian maturity, to the enlarging of her own organs.

This is Faulkner's purple prose at its most purple. He writes with all the stops pulled out. But it is effective. In passages such as this—and there are many of them in *The Hamlet*—Faulkner succeeds in creating the sense that Eula is a pagan goddess, one fit to follow in the train of the old Greek god Dionysus. Symbolically, she too, like Lena, signifies the vitality and power of the forces of nature, but in her the natural forces are etherialized. Eula is raised above the merely human. It is by the barest minimum that Faulkner manages to keep her credibly human.

—Cleanth Brooks, *On the Prejudices, Predilections, and Firm Beliefs of William Faulkner: Essays by Cleanth Brooks* (Baton Rouge: Louisiana State University Press, 1987): pp. 81–83

⊛

JUDITH BRYANT WITTENBERG ON WOMEN IN *LIGHT IN AUGUST*

[Judith Bryant Wittenberg is a professor of English at Simmons College. She is the author of *Faulkner: The Transfiguration of Biography*. In this excerpt, Wittenberg speaks on the general plight of women in the novel.]

In some respects, Faulkner's recognition of the general plight of women in the fictional world of *Light in August*—at once timeless and time-bound—makes it tempting to read the novel as proto-feminist. Byron Bunch, for example, comments on Hightower's obsession with his dead grandfather as an instance of the sort of unfortunate thing "that men do to the women who belong to them. . . . that is why women have to be strong and should not be held blameable for what they do with or for or because of men, since God knew that being anybody's wife was a tricky enough business," and the novel portrays throughout the difficulties encountered by all women who are in some sense belongings of the men they marry— or simply of a patriarchal society with rigid conceptions of women's essential nature and of what constitutes appropriate behavior in a female. Some of the men, such as Gail Hightower and Nathaniel Burden, see their wives solely as instruments of their own designs, paying no heed to the women's individual needs unless forced to do so; others, like Armstid, view their spouses from a wary distance with a mixture of fear and reluctant admiration. Virtually all of the men have strong ideas about "their" women and about women in general, and Faulkner sometimes depicts the operations of such thinking in ways that reveal a certain sympathy with its targets. So the contemporary Southern concept of virginity as necessary in an unmarried woman—a concept originating, as the psychoanalyst Karen Horney has pointed out, in the male wish to "ensure some measure of 'sexual thralldom'" in a wife-to-be—crumbles with ludicrous ease at the moment when Byron falls in love with the pregnant but single Lena Grove, "contrary to all the tradition of his austere and jealous country raising which demands in the object physical inviolability."

Although the veneration of virginity was openly restrictive, creating problems for any woman who willingly or inadvertently transgressed it, more subtle difficulties were engendered by such conventions as the praise of maternity. After seeing Lena with her newborn child, Hightower thinks of her admiringly, musing on the "young strong body from out whose travail even there shone something tranquil and unafraid" and on what he now sees as "*her life, her destiny. The good stock peopling in tranquil obedience to it the good earth; from these hearty loins without hurry or haste descending mother and daughter.*" Hightower's warm regard has a nether side, however, for he is tacitly circumscribing Lena's potential by viewing her as biologically determined: childbearing may be personally gratifying for a woman, even as it fulfills the need of the human race to perpetuate itself, but it is only one aspect of the female experience—as Lena herself seems to recognize when she seeks to evade or at least delay her female fate by engaging in travel and seeing the world. Although males are the principal proponents of ideas that overtly or implicitly limit the ways women are seen and permitted to behave, women themselves readily, if unconsciously, internalize them—like the "good women" of Jefferson who have "plenty of time to smell out sin" and thus are quick to condemn the peccadilloes of Hightower's wife. Faulkner's "good women" are characteristically those who have accepted patriarchal prescriptions, and their treatment of members of their own sex, as depicted in works like *Light in August* and *Sanctuary*, may be no less pernicious than the treatment women receive from men.

—Judith Bryant Wittenberg, "The Women of *Light in August*." In *New Essays on Light in August*, ed. Michael Millgate (Cambridge: Cambridge University Press, 1987): pp. 104–105

[Virginia V. James Hlavsa has taught English at Queens College, and has published extensively on Faulkner. Her articles and poetry have appeared in such publications as *Novel*, *American Literature*, and the *New York Times*. In this excerpt, Hlavsa discusses the mythical symbolism of Faulkner's characters.]

To uncover the challenges of *Light in August*, we should consider the book's anomalies. To begin with, one of the book's puzzles is that the many religious and mythical motifs appear to operate simultaneously. With names like Joanna Burden, Lena Grove, or Joe Christmas, we are almost in the world of Everyman, yet these characters do not stay in their assigned roles. Joanna resembles Diana, while Lena is an Earth Mother. But both have biblical associations, as well. Joanna, the feminine form of John, has the Baptist's initials, she appears before J. C., and her head is cut off. And despite the associations of "Lena" with Helena or Magdalena, this "lady" arrives wearing her madonna blue, bearing her "luck" (which might be her "election") and carrying her palm-leaf fan, along with her rather determined innocence. She is, in other words, a Mary. Well, the facts make clear that she is not. Is this a sly dig at the doctrine of the virgin birth or testimony to the possibility of genuine innocence despite actual guilt?

Joe Christmas is a similar puzzle. Like Christ, he has mysterious parentage, his feet are votively bathed, he appears to reject his mother (from John's "Woman, what have I to do with thee?"), he lives fifteen years in obscurity, he experiences an agony in the "ruined garden," and at 33 (or is it 36? Jesus' age is also only approximated [Luke 3:23]), he experiences a kind of crucifixion, complete with the five wounds, and a prompt apotheosis: "The man seemed to rise soaring into their memories forever and ever." But surely Joe cannot be Christ; no matter how we sympathize with his grim childhood (and who would suggest that Christ was the result of a poor upbringing), Joe is a murderer and, perhaps worse, a man of no message, at least none that *he* can articulate. Try as one might, despite one's intuition of a Christian connection, it is hard to give that connection shape and substance.

And of course, there are other puzzles. Recall the confusion, on first reading the novel, in the two contrasting depictions of Bobbie, from the wayward girl in chapter 8 to the screaming whore in chapter 9. Or recall, in chapter 4, that Hightower suddenly begins to sweat on hearing, not of the murder, but that Joe is "part nigger." Or recall Joe's odd behavior in chapter 5, slapping his drunken partner, "Joe Brown" (Lucas), or stripping himself before Joanna's window, or tramping off to the stable to "smell horses."

Real problems such as these have led critics to some odd conclusions. Ignore the omniscient author's description of Joe's life, which "for all its anonymous promiscuity, had been conventional enough, as a life of healthy and normal sin usually is," one critic suggests that Hightower and Joe had been homosexual partners. Another calls Christmas a "pervert" or a "sadomasochist." Another gives him an "inferiority complex." Strained as these suggestions are, they arise from our struggles to explain some bizarre behavior.

—Virginia V. James Hlavsa, *Faulkner and the Thoroughly Modern Novel* (Charlottesville: University of Virginia Press, 1991): pp. 21–23

Plot Summary of
The Sound and the Fury

The novel opens in the first-person perspective of a 33-year-old mentally handicapped man named Benjy Compson. Faulkner has divided the novel into four chapters, each titled by a specific date and each narrated from the first-person perspective of one of the characters, with the exception of the fourth and final chapter, which is narrated in the third person. The narrative is clearly non-linear, as evidenced by the chapter titles: "April Seventh, 1928," "June Second, 1910," "April Sixth, 1928," and "April Eighth, 1928." With the exception of the fourth section, the narrative is largely stream-of-consciousness, the prose style varying with each character.

Faulkner opens (**April Seventh, 1928**) with the most obscure and challenging chapter, presented from the scattered and scarcely cohesive perspective of Benjy. The story begins along the border of a golf course where Benjy is accompanied by Luster, a black family servant. Luster is searching for a quarter that fell through a hole in his pocket. The sound of Benjy's sobbing—his reaction to a great many events—recurs throughout the novel, as each character reveals his or her own interpretation of what Benjy's howls mean.

As with other sections of the novel, Benjy spends less time in the present than he does "flashing" back to past events. Because of his mental deficiency, the transitions and the individual circumstances are difficult to track. Not until the same events are presented in later chapters from different perspectives does the reader begin to piece together the chronology of the four primary days of the novel.

Benjy's recollections are usually associated with smell or its absence, such as the outdoor, tree-like smell of Caddy. A great deal of his reflection is centered around Caddy, whose promiscuity and rebellion are at the heart of the disintegration of the Compson family. Caddy is the most meaningful character in Benjy's life, even after she is banished from the family. She is the only one who is consistently sympathetic toward Benjy and who seems to understand the reasons for his outbursts.

One of the central events of the Benjy section that recurs throughout the novel takes place on the evening that Damuddy, the grandmother of Benjy and his siblings, dies. Earlier in the day, Benjy, Caddy, Quentin, Jason, and an old family servant named Versh have gathered at the river. Caddy and Quentin get into a water fight, during which Quentin pushes Caddy into the mud and she dirties her dress. When they return to the house later that night, fearful that they will get in trouble for arriving home dirty and wet, they are told the news about their grandmother.

Another focal point in the novel is Caddy's wedding. Benjy's strongest memories are sharing an excessive amount of sarsaparilla with T. P., one of the Compson's old servants, and becoming profoundly ill. The reader discovers in Quentin's section that Caddy was pregnant at her wedding and uncertain who the father was. Caddy gives birth to a baby girl whom she names after her brother, Quentin, who drowned himself after her wedding and before the child was born.

The next chapter, **June Second, 1910,** is told from Quentin Compson's point of view. It covers the events in Quentin's last day of life, the day he commits suicide. Here the reader gains additional information about the major events in the Compson family's life. The primary difference between the first and second narratives is that Quentin's departures from the present are clearly marked by his heightened awareness of time—a concept unrecognizable to Benjy. While in his Harvard dorm room, Quentin's thoughts shift from his ability to tell time based on a shadow on the curtains, to the watch that his father gave him, to his father's theories on time, and finally to the sound of the watch itself; a sound that haunts Quentin throughout his final day. This attention to time acts not only as a recurring theme within Quentin's narrative but also as a strong distinguishing characteristic dividing Quentin's narrative from Benjy's.

Like Benjy, Quentin's focus is also on his sister Caddy, but in a different way. When she loses her virginity, he contemplates claiming to have had an incestuous relationship with her to somehow preserve her honor. He takes responsibility for Caddy's behavior, which ultimately leads to her banishment from the family. Quentin also dwells on his relationship with his father, whose darkly cynical views on life and the manner in which he drank himself to death are inescapable elements of Quentin's psyche.

Quentin spends some time preparing for his suicide. He dresses in his finest clothes, then composes two suicide notes, which he addresses to Shreve, his college roommate and friend. He makes arrangements to have them delivered to him the following day. He takes his broken watch to a hardware store, though he does not want to get it fixed. Quentin's thoughts turn intermittently back to the water fight he had with Caddy on the evening of his grandmother's death. He believes that Benjy was able to smell when their grandmother died. He also seems haunted by the fact that his parents sold Benjy's pasture to finance his Harvard education. This fact is revisited in Jason's narrative, pitting Quentin's guilt and sadness over the sale against Jason's bitterness that he was not the recipient of such generosity.

The events of Quentin's last day take a peculiar turn, beginning with an interaction with three boys who are fishing for trout, hoping to win a $25 prize. The boys eventually decide to forsake the fishing and go swimming instead. As Quentin wanders through town physically, his mind meanders in and out of the past. (Faulkner indicates shifts between present time and the past with typeface: italics for the past and Roman type for the present.) He enters a general store, where he buys a bun for himself and a little girl who followed him in. His attempts to get her to speak are unsuccessful, so he leads her to a drugstore, where he buys her ice cream. Although he tries to find out where she lives, she still will not speak, so he goes on his way. He soon discovers that she is following him, so he tries to find out where she lives. Eventually, two men see Quentin with the girl and, believing he is abducting her, one attacks Quentin and pummels his face until the other man pulls him off. The men take Quentin to the local jail, where he pays a dollar to the men and six dollars to the court to secure his release.

Following this incident, Quentin runs into his roommate, Shreve, along with Gerald and Spoade, acquaintances from Harvard. Throughout their interaction, Quentin's thoughts shift back and forth between musings on his own virginity and memories of Caddy. He relives an encounter with Caddy which took place at a tree outside of the family house. At the time, Quentin suggested that they commit a double suicide, and said that he would cut his sister's throat with a knife. He cut his own, but though Caddy claimed to be willing, Quentin could not go through with it. His mind then turns to the night Caddy lost her virginity, remembering how Benjy had tried to clean the foreign smell from her. He remembers how he threatened Dalton Ames, the man who took Caddy's innocence, and his emotions bring him back to the present, to the uncontrollable anger he feels toward Gerald, whom Quentin believes to be a liar and a chauvinist. Quentin strikes the much larger and stronger Gerald, who retaliates and beats him to the ground, bloodying his suit.

Quentin's section ends as he meticulously prepares for his suicide. First, he returns to his dorm, where he cleans the blood stains from his clothes. He gathers his goods and makes sure that he has the letters for his roommate. On his way out, he remembers that he has neglected to brush his teeth. The chapter ends as he remembers to also brush his hat. The reader is left to believe that this will be his final act before he makes his way to the river, where he has hidden weights that he will attach to himself before jumping into the water.

The third chapter, **April Sixth, 1928,** is told from the point of view of Jason, the brother of Quentin, Benjy, and Caddy, and the antithesis of Quentin. Faulkner allows us to see his nature immediately in the opening line of the chapter: "Once a bitch always a bitch," he claims. Although Jason's section is also a stream-of-consciousness narrative, this section differs from the previous two in that he is concerned only with the present and rarely contemplates the past. Jason is consumed by spite and bitterness, and he directs the majority of his anger toward his niece Quentin, Caddy's daughter. Caddy has been banished from the household, forbidden to see her daughter. Jason is so consumed by Quentin's ungratefulness and misbehavior that he resorts to following her around town to see what she is doing and with whom.

Caddy sends checks for her daughter's support, but Jason steals them and keeps the money for himself. He then creates false checks, which he gives to his mother so that she can burn them to feel as though she is refusing Caddy's money. Jason wants to be considered head of the household; the provider and thus the controller of everyone's lives. His mother, weak and vain, supports his claim. He works at a store for a man named Earl, and during the day he constantly leaves the store to attend to dishonest business of his own.

A letter arrives from Caddy that accuses Jason of reading her letters and withholding her money from Quentin. Jason's mind is perpetually consumed by the acts of his niece and the money, which he has invested in stocks. His prejudice is evident throughout this chapter, largely from his statements toward the help and his incessant remarks about the money-hoarding Jews who control the stock market.

In the Jason section, the reader also learns more details about the death and funeral of Jason Compson III, the father of Benjy, Jason, Quentin, and Caddy. Caddy shows up at the funeral, even though she has been banished from the household, and approaches Jason about seeing her daughter, who was taken from her soon after the child was born. Jason agrees to let Caddy see her daughter after she gives him $100 in cash. Jason tells her where to meet, and then, cruelly, drives a carriage quickly past Caddy while he holds up her baby in the window. Caddy appears at the store where Jason works and accuses him of lying and being coldhearted. After she leaves, Jason realizes that she probably went to the house to see her daughter, and in an angry fit, drives home and berates Dilsey, the black nanny, threatening to sell her if she ever allows Caddy in the house again.

Now at the store in the present time, Jason opens a letter from Caddy that contains a money order for her daughter. She has arranged it so that Quentin needs to sign the money order to keep Jason from appropriating the money for himself. Quentin shows up at the store expecting the money from her mother and Jason manipulates her into signing the check, giving her 10 dollars in exchange— the amount that he claims is the full value of the money order. After conjuring a fake check from an old company checkbook, Jason drives home and lets his mother burn what she believes to be Caddy's money. Also in the mail that day was a letter from uncle Maury—Jason's mother's brother—asking for money. Though Jason clearly resents this sponging uncle, his mother remains blindly sympathetic to her wayward brother.

When Jason returns to the store, Earl expresses his displeasure with Jason's absence. He tells Jason that he knows Jason's mother has given him power of attorney and that he also knows that Jason is swindling her. He also says that he's aware that Jason's mother believes that he has $1,000 invested in the store—the same amount Earl believes Jason has used to buy his car. As the conversation winds down, Jason sees Quentin walking past the store with a man in a red tie. He springs out the door and attempts to determine which way they were heading. He decides to drive back to the house to see if Quentin was on her way home. On his return trip, he sees Quentin in a car with the man, speeding down the street. He tracks them down and finds the empty car parked in a clearing off the road. He parks next to the car and searches in the woods for them. When he gets back to his car, they've returned to their car and have taken off, howling out the window. He quickly discovers that they have let the air out of his tires.

After borrowing a pump, Jason once again returns to the store where he gets into another argument with Earl. As the day winds down, he buys a few cigars at a local store and heads home. Luster, one of the servants (who was seen searching for his quarter in the opening scene of the novel), is talking about his lack of money and his desire to see the traveling show that has come to town. Jason reveals that he has two free tickets he's not going to use, though he refuses to give them away. When Luster pleads with Jason to give him one of the tickets, Jason burns them in the stove.

The fourth and final chapter of the book takes place two days after the Jason section, **April Eighth, 1928**, Easter Sunday. The chapter is narrated in the third person, focusing primarily on Dilsey, the black servant in the Compson household. Dilsey is getting the house in order before attending Easter services. She is behind in her ritual duties because Luster, who made it to the show the previous night, overslept and did not do his chores.

When Jason, Caroline, Benjy, and Luster are downstairs, Jason reveals that the window in his room has been broken. He declares that since he had the locks changed, he has the only key to the room and that no one has access inside. When Dilsey is nearly done preparing breakfast, Jason decides that he wants Quentin to come downstairs for breakfast, despite the fact that she usually sleeps in on Sundays. As Dilsey stands outside Quentin's door, calling for her to come to breakfast, and Jason and his mother discuss the broken window, Mrs. Compson makes the statement: "It's just as if somebody had tried to break into the house," causing Jason to spring up from his seat and flee up the stairs, realizing that it was probably Quentin who broke the window. After forcing Dilsey to relinquish her keys, he opens the door to Quentin's room and discovers that she is gone. Jason then realizes that she has stolen his secret stash of money. He calls the police and tells them that he has been robbed, but when he does not get the reaction he expects from the police, he storms out of the house and heads to the station himself. Luster then reveals that he and Benjy saw Quentin climb out that window the night before.

In an attempt to get things back to normal, Dilsey cleans the house and prepares herself for church. Luster also retreats to his quarters and comes back dressed for the Easter service. They leave the house and walk to church, meeting fellow worshippers along the way. The sermon given by a visiting minister causes Dilsey to weep.

Now at the police station, Jason tries to persuade a police officer that they must leave immediately to track down the thieves who broke into his house. The officer claims that unless he has substantial proof of who took Jason's money, he cannot take any action. Jason leaves in a fit of anger and heads for Mottstown, where the traveling show is scheduled to stop, suspecting that Quentin has run off with the man in the red tie, a member of the show. Confronting an elderly man, Jason insists that he tell him where his niece has gone. The man attacks Jason, causing him to fall back on his head. After Jason is resuscitated, it is revealed that the show director had turned Quentin and the man in the red tie away. Jason then hires someone to drive him back to Jefferson.

The novel concludes as Luster is driving Benjy around in the horse-drawn carriage. Each time Luster veers from course slightly, Benjy screams. By this time, Jason has made it back to town, where he sees the carriage and hears Benjy screaming, leading him to hurl Luster out of the way and turn the carriage around, because he does not want anyone in town to see his brother. The novels ends with the sound of horses calming Benjy down. ✿

List of Characters in
The Sound and the Fury

Caddy Compson is the central figure in the novel. She is closely connected to virtually every major event, while also existing as a common point of reference in each of the four narratives comprising the book. She named her daughter after her brother Quentin, who committed suicide soon after her marriage.

Benjy Compson is the mentally handicapped brother of Caddy, Quentin, and Jason. The first chapter of the book is a first-person "narrative" from his perspective, taking place on his 33rd birthday.

Quentin Compson, the narrator of the second section, is a Harvard student whose family sold Benjy's pasture to pay for his education. He blames himself for the loss of his sister's innocence, and his resulting despair is a contributing factor in his decision to commit suicide.

Jason Compson IV is the narrator of the third section. Selfishness, bitterness, and anger dictate most of his thoughts and actions. He is head of the Compson household during the family's final disintegration.

Dilsey Gibson is the black nanny who is the central character in the fourth and final chapter. As one of the few rational characters in the story, she is a stabilizing figure in the novel.

Miss Quentin is Caddy's daughter, named after her mother's brother who committed suicide. Miss Quentin is at odds with her uncle Jason throughout the last half of the novel.

Caroline Bascomb Compson is the mother of Benjy, Caddy, Quentin, and Jason. A self-centered, mean-spirited woman, she allows her son Jason to run the Compson household and is responsible for banishing Caddy from the family.

Jason Compson III is the father of Caddy, Benjy, Quentin, and Jason. His cynicism is woven throughout the book, especially in the Quentin section.

Maury Bascomb, Caroline's brother, is an alcoholic who lives off the Compson family's money.

Luster is a black servant who looks after Benjy. ✤

Critical Views on
The Sound and the Fury

RICHARD P. ADAMS ON THE CENTRAL CHARACTER IN
THE SOUND AND THE FURY

[Richard P. Adams (1917–1977) began teaching at Rutgers
University in 1947. He published various articles and
books including *Faulkner: Myth and Motion*. In this
excerpt, Adams discusses Caddy Compson as the germ of
Faulkner's novel.]

The Sound and the Fury contained, according to Faulkner's draft
introduction, "perhaps the only thing in literature which would ever
move me very much: Caddy climbing the pear tree to look in the
window at her grandmother's funeral while Quentin and Jason and
Benjy and the negroes looked up at the muddy seat of her drawers."
Later, in interviews, Faulkner consistently said that his conception of
the book had grown from this germ. When someone at Virginia
asked about his "impression" of the girl in the tree, Faulkner
objected that "impression is the wrong word. It's more an image, a
very moving image to me was of the children. 'Course, we didn't
know at that time that one was an idiot, but they were three boys,
one was a girl and the girl was the only one that was brave enough to
climb that tree to look in the forbidden window to see what was
going on. And that's what the book—and it took the rest of the four
hundred pages to explain why she was brave enough to climb the
tree to look in the window. It was an image, a picture to me, a very
moving one, which was symbolized by the muddy bottom of her
drawers as her brothers looked up into the apple tree that she had
climbed to look in the window. And the symbolism of the muddy
bottom of the drawers became the lost Caddy. . . ." Perhaps "explain"
is not the right word either, for the story does not explain Caddy's
bravery, and Faulkner never, in or out of the story, explained why the
"image" fascinated him so. But he did make it clear that the whole
book is an effort to focus the looking of the other children—and
thereby the reader—at "the muddy bottom of the drawers" of a girl
who only later became sufficiently abstracted from the "image" to
acquire a name and a fate.

The image associates a girl with a tree, as Faulkner's early work does, but with more ambiguity. Caddy is in one aspect a dryad, and to Benjy she usually smells like trees. But she is not virginal like the poplars of the early poems. She is more the Arician Diana, going to meet her lover Dalton Ames among the trees, like Addie and Dewey Dell Bundren, or Lena Grove. Even at the age of seven she climbs a fertile fruit tree, like those in *Soldiers' Pay, Sartoris,* and *The Hamlet;* and already her drawers are stained with symbolic mud, making Faulkner's usual association of fecundity with foulness. In another aspect she is like Eve, seeking forbidden knowledge, which happens to be knowledge of death. Perhaps that is why Faulkner remembered the tree as an apple in the interview, which took place in 1957, although he had remembered it as a pear in the draft introduction, written about 1932 or 1933. Perhaps that is also why we are told that "A snake crawled out from under the house" just before Caddy climbs the tree, and why a few minutes later Dilsey says to her, "'You, Satan. . . . Come down from there.'"

—Richard P. Adams, *Faulkner: Myth and Motion* (Princeton: Princeton University Press, 1968): pp. 217–219

LINDA W. WAGNER ON CADDY COMPSON'S IMPORTANCE TO BENJY

[Linda W. Wagner has taught at Michigan State University and the University of North Carolina. Her writings include *"The Age of Innocence": A Novel of Ironic Nostalgia* and *Telling Women's Lives: The New Biography.* In this excerpt, Wagner discusses Caddy Compson as central to the "Benjy Section" of the novel.]

Faulkner structurally has shaped the Benjy section of *The Sound and the Fury* so that Caddy's presence or absence does create or diminish Benjy's life. The first scene in this kaleidoscope of visual images is that of the golfers approaching Benjy across the former Compson pasture. The first spoken language in the novel is "Here, caddie." With the mention of Caddy's name, Benjy's own sound begins. (We do not hear it, but everyone else in range does: "'Listen at you, now.'

Luster said. 'Ain't you something, thirty-three years old, going on that way. . . .'" So important was the mention of Caddy to be that in the manuscript version of this scene Faulkner did not include Benjy's age or the fact that it is his birthday: the only reason for this initial scene is to show Benjy's reaction to the sound of Caddy's name. (In the manuscript version, Caddie is capitalized when the golfer speaks the word.)

The first scene, then, gives us Benjy's lament, and his lament is not for the downfall of the Compson family or lineage but—much more directly and personally—for the loss of Caddy. The first flashback, a structural decision of equal import as to what will be the opening scene, is of Caddy and Benjy together, doing something as equals, with Caddy instructing Benjy. The second flashback is Benjy waiting by the gate for Caddy, a poignantly charged image, for we see him often—fenced in, captive, waiting for a release that never comes. Because Caddy, and Caddy's ability to reach Benjy through language, might have saved Benjy from his tragic fate of inaction, her loss is the most important single happening of the novel.

The scene of Benjy's waiting for Caddy also shows Benjy's ability to manipulate the family. He has gotten himself outside in time to meet her; without language, he has conveyed his needs well enough that people have responded. Caddy is his motivation. We see very few acts on Benjy's part throughout the novel; by the present time of the book he is cast only as a reactor, and his chief reaction is to mourn. When he was a child, however, Benjy did show initiative.

In these early scenes, Faulkner also shows the advantage of Caddy's responsible behavior toward Benjy. She knows what the child means, wants, and feels. Others in the family do not, partly because they do not communicate directly with him. When Mrs. Compson wants information about Benjy, she asks Versh instead of Benjy: "'Is he cold, Versh?'" A simple touch would have told her; instead she receives false information. Mrs. Compson talks *at* Benjy (as she later talks at Jason, Quentin, and Dilsey), but she does not listen: speech for her is monologue, self-aggrandisement. Her "sympathy" for Benjy, in the most loving scene between her and her young retarded son, is all self-pity.

—Linda W. Wagner, "Language and Act: Caddy Compson." In *The Southern Literary Journal* XIV, no. 2 (Spring 1982): pp. 52–53

[Eric J. Sundquist is a professor of English at the University of California at Berkeley. His works include *Home as Found: Authority and Genealogy in Nineteenth-Century American Literature* and *Faulkner: The House Divided,* from which this excerpt is taken.]

The Sound and the Fury begins in the mind of an idiot. Faulkner's detractors have suggested that once he discovered this impossible world he never left it, that Benjy Compson is, ironically, his one great creation, or, at best, that the novel is a fine modernist experiment unrivaled by following novels, in which Faulkner became obsessed with white Negroes and the like. This is at least half wrong, for *The Sound and the Fury* is not Faulkner's best novel, but the paradox is this: its importance only appears in the larger context of novels to which it gives rise, and at that point it comes to seem indispensable. Here again the question is genetic, so to speak, for the novel is demonstrably about failed integrity—in the Compson family, the Southern dream, the novel as a conventional form, and the "mind" of the author. All of these issues, rightly enough, appear to converge in the mind of Benjy, and the rest of the novel is a slow extraction of attention from this originating abyss. Such a narrative development produces paradoxical effects that bear on, and reappear in, all of Faulkner's work, but their most salient feature in this case is a thorough devaluation of traditional novelistic plot or action.

Nearly everything that "happens" in the novel happens in the first section—and this is exactly what Faulkner, who largely created for readers the idolatrous admiration of Caddy Compson they have expressed, asks us to believe. The genetic myth of the novel—that "it began with the picture of the little girl's muddy drawers, climbing that tree to look in the parlor window" at her grandmother's funeral—had so overwhelmed the novel itself that one no longer questions its relevance, even though there is good reason to do so. One might rather say that his scene stands in the same relation to Caddy as Caddy does to the entire novel, for we find out so little about her that we might conclude, on the basis of the action of the novel, either that she is a tender-hearted tramp or that, because she is surrounded by every conceivable form of mental and emotional instability, her own actions are justifiably inevitable. But since Caddy is not a character but an idea, an obsession in the minds of her brothers, we cannot rightly be said to find out much about her. Caddy is "lost" psychologically and aesthetically as well as morally: she is the very symbol of loss in Faulkner's world—the loss of innocence, integrity, chronology, personality, and dramatic unity, all the problematic virtues of his envisioned artistic design. To Benjy she smells like trees, to Quentin she is would-be lover, to Jason she is the whore mother of a whore daughter, and to Faulkner she is at once "the sister which I did not have and the daughter which I was to lose," and "a beautiful and tragic little girl" who later becomes, apparently, the mistress of a Nazi officer in occupied France. There is probably no major character in literature about whom we know so little in proportion to the amount of attention she receives. This is surely no objection to the novel, but it is quite certainly a measure of its drama, which is submerged to the point of invisibility.

> —Eric J. Sundquist, *Faulkner: The House Divided* (Baltimore: Johns Hopkins University Press, 1983): pp. 9–10

(b)

KENZABURO OHASHI ON CHARACTER TYPES IN FAULKNER'S NOVELS

[Kenzaburo Ohashi is a professor of American Literature at Tsurami University. Her works include *Man and the World: Essays on American Literature,* and a three volume study of William Faulkner. In this excerpt, Ohashi examines the parallels between characters in *The Sound and the Fury* and those of Faulkner's other novels.]

William Faulkner seems often to have broadened and deepened his imaginative world by parodying his own creations, or, at least, by repeating them in his own unique way. In portraying Eula Varner of *The Hamlet,* for example, he parodied, either consciously or unconsciously, or at least repeated self-consciously, the characterization of Caddy (Candace) Compson of *The Sound and the Fury.* Caddy had an illegitimate daughter (Quentin), just as Eula has one who will be known as Linda later in *The Town* and *The Mansion.* Whereas Miss

Quentin's father is unknown, Linda's is definitely Hoake McCarron, a young man with a "bold and handsome" face, who, having come courting Eula from outside the hamlet of Frenchman's Bend and swiftly gaining what he wanted, fled away "not only from Frenchman's Bend but from the country itself . . . because of what he believed the Varner men would do," much as Dalton Ames, who came to Jefferson as a stranger, went abruptly away after gaining both Caddy's heart and body, leaving Quentin Compson impotent and frustrated in his failure to protect his sister.

Moreover, compare this Quentin Compson with Jody Varner, Eula's brother, who when he knows of Eula's pregnancy tries to run after McCarron in order to catch and kill him with an ancient pistol that belonged to his great-grandfather; stopped by his father, who is old and thin against the son's youth and two hundred pounds, Jody screams impotently about the family's "name." Faulkner could no more have written these several pages of *The Hamlet* without recalling Quentin Compson of *The Sound and the Fury* than he could have described Eula as a schoolgirl with "the tawdry oilcloth receptacle that was obviously a grammar-school book-satchel" without having Caddy in mind again as a small girl running with her book-satchel swinging behind to meet Benjy at the gate of the Compson house. The recalling may not have been deliberate, but certainly it was there.

In *The Hamlet* there is another instance of resemblance to *The Sound and the Fury*, which not only echoes the words used in the Compson novel but is also closely related to the Eula-Caddy and Jody-Quentin parallels, at least in thematic significance. Ike Snopes, who like Benjy is an idiot, speaks to the cow he loves, "moaning a little, urgent and concerned yet not to alarm her more," touches her with this hand, "speaking to her again, murmurous, drooling," and later follows her a second time, "trying to tell her how this violent violation of her maiden's delicacy is no shame, since such is the very iron imperishable warp of the fabric of love." Just so Benjy tried to "tell" Caddy, and later to "say" to the girls who were passing the Compson gate coming home from school (to say what, we do not exactly know). There are of course many differences between the two stories. First, Ike has no blood relation with the Varners as Benjy has with the Compsons, and the object of his love is not a human being but an animal. By far the most important difference is that whereas

Benjy moans after a lost Caddy and never gains his love back, Ike, though he moans "a little, urgent and concerned," is so self-confident as to try to tell the cow something about "love" and thus finally attains the fulfillment of his urgent desire. These differences enrich the picture of human life in the county of Yoknapatawpha and give it wider and deeper dimensions through that contrast and repetition. Furthermore, no irony or parody, as such, of the Compson material is intended—no irony that might arise, for example, out of such a paradoxical contrast as that between the lost love of the idiot Benjy toward a sister and the gained love of the idiot Ike toward a cow. Rather than a denial, a forgetting or ignoring of the previous version by mere humorous repetition of a similar theme and pattern of story, this is nothing if not an enrichment of the world already created, a presentation of new possibilities in that world through a unique repetition or self-parody. A new and rich world of comedy concerning human love is presented in *The Hamlet,* set against the tragic aspects of love presented symbolically in the novel written more than ten years earlier.

—Kenzaburo Ohashi, "Creation through Repetition or Self-Parody." In *Faulkner Studies in Japan*, ed. Thomas L. McHaney (Athens, GA: University of Georgia Press, 1985): pp. 15–17

✌

DAVID DOWLING ON QUENTIN COMPSON

[David Dowling teaches the Modern Novel at Massey University, New Zealand, and is the editor for *Landfall,* a literary quarterly. His writings include *Fictions of Nuclear Disaster.* In this excerpt, Dowling examines the contradictions in Quentin Compson's character.]

If Benjy's section is the first movement of Faulkner's symphony sounding the themes and fitfully developing them, then Quentin's section is the slow dance. He is described in Faulkner's Appendix:

Who loved not his sister's body but some concept of Compson honour precariously and (he knew well) only temporarily supported by the minute fragile membrane of her maidenhead as a miniature replica of all the whole vast globy earth may be poised on the nose of a trained seal. Who loved not the idea of the incest which he would not commit, but some presbyterian concept of its eternal punishment. . . . But who loved death above all, who loved only death. . . .

Quentin's speech appears normal but he is as insulated from the present as his brother Benjy, particularly during the recollection of two primal scenes: his fight with Caddy's boyfriend and the events of that day; and his interview with his father. In the latter he reduces himself to silent insignificance—'and I temporary.' The section begins with dawn and his falling 'in time again', and ends with his preparations to exit from time forever. The shadow (first noun of his section) which haunts him is his own mortality, which he identifies with his sister's pre-sexual being. He is 'but a walking shadow' for whom, in a terrifyingly complete inverse logic, life is death, Caddy's sexual flowering a fall into decay, and time an outrage to be stopped at all costs, either by smashing a watch or taking one's own life. He even wishes he could have been his own father's father, or Dalton Ames's mother, to put a stop to the absurd cycle of procreation.

However, Faulkner carefully indicates that Quentin is closer to normalcy than these feverish moments might suggest. At breakfast he forgets about time and then has to excuse himself for his lapse; he is aware of his own neurosis, and spends much of the day doing normal things. Even though he greets the little girl at the bakery with 'Hello sister', he treats her with genuine kindness. He might have been sustained by the kind of aristocratic 'morality' which he sees in Gerald and his mother, as he rows down the river and she travels in grand isolation but parallel to him. But Mrs Compson has abdicated, offering no resistance to Mr Compson's misogyny which, in combination with Quentin's genuine love for his sister, becomes an intolerable contradiction: women, the one possible escape from Mr Compson's bleak, nihilistic world, are bitches.

—David Dowling, *William Faulkner* (London: Macmillan Publishers, 1989): pp. 45–46

KARL F. ZENDER ON TEACHING AND LEARNING IN THE SOUND AND THE FURY

[Karl F. Zender is a professor of English at the University of California at Davis. He has published many articles and essays on Faulkner, and is co-author of *Persuasive Writing: A College Reader*. Here, Zender discusses the concept of instructing and learning in Faulkner's novel.]

Faulkner's critique of parenthood renders problematic the idea of instruction. However indirectly, most teaching involves a transfer of power between generations and therefore presupposes the existence of altruistic impulses in the teacher and of a willingness to learn in the pupil. In part of his being, Quentin desperately wants such a transfer to take place. Beneath his metaphysical pretensions he is an adolescent, with an adolescent's characteristic mixture of desire for adult capacities and of embarrassment over not already possessing them; and throughout the last day of his life he displays a continual, although sidelong, interest in the ways his contemporaries are making the transition into adulthood. Looking out his dormitory window at students hurrying to chapel, he reflects on Spoade's casual, "senior" attitude—so unlike his own—toward the college's rules and regulations. Although not a smoker, he buys a cigar after breakfast and tries to smoke it; later in the day he recalls in precise and envious detail Dalton Ames's ability to roll a cigarette, to strike a match with his thumb, and to blow smoke through his nose. Returning to the dormitory after his fight with Gerald Bland, he displays an agonized adolescent self-consciousness in the steps he takes to prevent people from seeing his black eye; and in the last act we see him perform, he pauses to put on his hat before leaving to commit suicide so that other students won't think he is "a Harvard Square student making like he was a senior."

This distaste for adolescence and desire for adult power and knowledge helps to explain why Quentin so frequently envisions his father in the role of instructor and himself in the role of student. Throughout his recollections of their conversations, he assiduously attends to his father's apothegms and explanations, as if hoping to learn from them the secrets of adulthood. Yet in another and more dominant part of his personality, Quentin deeply distrusts all education. His sense of the inauthenticity of his parents' lives combines with his fear of time and sexuality to create a despairing sense that learning the lessons of adulthood will destroy, rather than deepen, the meaning of his existence. He views education, in its public, institutional forms, as a source not of liberation but of repression, and he resists it internally even while outwardly displaying the characteristics of a good student. Of his childhood schooling he remembers only his almost erotic longing for the schoolday's end, and he is so indifferent to the educational aspects of his Harvard experience as to fail to mention any professors he has known, classes he has taken, or knowledge he has gained. And in his relation with his father, a similar undermining takes place. Although he assigns his father the role of instructor and himself the role of student, he tries to restrict the lesson he will learn to the circuit of his own backward-turning desire, demanding that his father teach him only how to be free of the need to be taught. Thus the conversation that dominates Quentin's memory just before he leaves the dormitory room for the last time takes on the quality of a mock tutorial, in which instruction is offered but rejected: "you are still blind," says Mr. Compson, "to what is in yourself to that part of general truth the sequence of natural events and their causes which shadows every mans brow even Benjys"; to which Quentin replies, sullenly, "nobody knows what i know."

—Karl F. Zender, *The Crossing of the Ways: William Faulkner, the South, and the Modern World* (New Brunswick, Rutgers University Press, 1989): pp. 114–15

⊛

MINROSE C. GWIN ON CADDY'S PRESENCE IN MALE DISCOURSE

[Minrose C. Gwin is a professor of English and Women's Studies at Virginia Polytechnic Institute and State University. She is the author of *Black and White Women of the Old South: The Peculiar Sisterhood in American Literature* and *The Feminine and Faulkner: Reading (Beyond) Sexual Difference*, from which this excerpt is taken.]

What we seek in seeking Caddy Compson is not only the language and force and mystery of woman within Faulkner's text and consciousness. This is also an inquiry into the nature of female subjectivity within a male text and the relationship of that subjectivity to what language can and cannot say. *The Sound and the Fury* itself asks the questions posed by Maurice Merleau-Ponty: "But what if language speaks as much by what is between words as by the words themselves? As much by what it does not 'say' as by what it 'says'?" Caddy's ability to speak to us as she traverses the spaces between presence and absence, text and nontext, the conscious and the unconscious, stretches our sense of the urgency of these questions. Simultaneously, her ability to play creatively within the bounded text of male discourse expands our sense of female energy and power, of its pressure upon the productivity of that text. Often we feel that Caddy isn't where we think she is, that her space is *somewhere else.* She is continually arising from and fading into her brothers' discourse, always in the process of emerging and disappearing in the male text. Her subjectivity, as the "punctuation" of the male discourse which bounds it, is always on the brink of *aphanisis,* fading and being lost. It thus speaks out of the play of presence and absence, moving up and down the pear tree, in and out of that hazy area between the conscious and the unconscious. As Régis Durand points out, Lacan has shown us that texts may be seen as existing around "the living moment" of the fading of the subject. Benjy's final musings are indeed so strangely moving, I suggest, because they allow us to feel almost simultaneously *both* the epiphany within the maternal space created between himself and Caddy *and* its *aphanisis:*

> Father went to the door and looked at us again. Then the dark came back, and he stood black in the door, and then the door turned black again. Caddy held me and I could hear us all, and the darkness, and something I could smell. And then I could see the windows, where the trees were buzzing. Then the dark began to go in smooth, bright shapes, like it always does, even when Caddy says that I have been asleep.

And yet the paradox is that Caddy *won't* fade completely; her voice and her presence emerge and reemerge throughout the narrative. She will not leave us; she rushes out of the mirror of male discourse, smelling like rain, offering Benjy's box of stars, speaking to us the language of creative play, of *différance,* of endless deconstruction and generation. Or grieving in a black raincoat, she appears suddenly out of nowhere on the periphery of the text, saying . . . what?

> —Minrose C. Gwin, *The Feminine and Faulkner: Reading (Beyond) Sexual Difference* (Knoxville: University of Tennessee Press, 1990): pp. 37–38

⊚

Noel Polk on the Mechanics of Language in *The Sound and the Fury*

[Noel Polk is a professor of English at the University of Southern Mississippi. He is the author of *A Study of William Faulkner's "Requiem for a Nun"* and the editor of a book of essays on Faulkner, from which this excerpt is taken.]

One of the great achievements of *The Sound and the Fury* is that in a novel which most critics now agree is centrally concerned with language, in a novel three of whose sections are "monologues" that make some gesture toward orality, Faulkner turns the clumsy mechanics of the representation of that language on paper, what Stephen Ross calls "the visual discourse of our reading," into a highly expressive part of the language itself. At one very simple level, reading, especially the reading of dialogue, involves translating one sense impression into another: the author translates the aural into the visual, readers translate the visual back into the aural—or should, if they want to understand *The Sound and the Fury.* For just as he plays with Benjy's hearing of the phonemes [*kædl*], so does Faulkner play with the way we read, with the mechanical signs of punctuation and spelling that harness and control, that give rhythm and shape and weight and expressive meaning to, the silent words that appear on the paper. Throughout the novel he uses an inventive array of visual devices in punctuation—or the lack of it—and spelling and grammar to help us focus on the way we comprehend language, written and oral.

Each brother, Judith Lockyer argues, "reveals an aspect of the power in language. That power is born out of the relation of language to consciousness." I would suggest more: Faulkner uses the mechanics of the English language—grammar, syntax, punctuation, spelling—as a direct objective correlative to the states of each of the narrators' minds. The mechanical conventions of the writing, then, sometimes work *against the words themselves,* so that they reveal things other than what the characters are saying; they work, in fact, to reveal things that the narrators are incapable of saying or are specifically trying to keep from saying, things that have caused them pain and shame. Words are, for Quentin and Jason at any rate, lids they use to seal that pain in the unconscious, though it constantly insist on verbalizing itself. We have access to their pain largely through what they *don't* say, and also through the visual forms of the language in which Faulkner has inscribed their thoughts and feelings on paper. Benjy's section prepares us powerfully for the much more complex linguistic situations in the next three sections.

Faulkner captures the disrelatedness of Benjy's various perceptions by drastically simplifying the referentiality and the mechanics of his language. ⟨. . .⟩

Many have noted that Benjy is "pre-lingual," that he "could never really narrate his section" because he has no language. But he is in fact *non*lingual: the language of the Benjy section is *Faulkner's* language. Properly speaking, Benjy is not a narrator at all, but the "very negation of narrative." ⟨. . .⟩ he is merely a filter, and not necessarily an ordering one, for the thousands of sense impressions he processes every day, which may remain just as confusing for him as they do for readers.

—Noel Polk, "Trying Not to Say: A Primer on the Language of *The Sound and the Fury.*" In *New Essays on The Sound and the Fury,* ed. Noel Polk (Cambridge: Cambridge University Press, 1993): pp. 143–44

⟨℣⟩

MICHAEL MILLGATE ON QUENTIN COMPSON AS A RECURRING CHARACTER IN FAULKNER'S WORKS

[Michael Millgate is a professor of English at the University of Toronto, where he has taught since 1967. He has authored or edited more than 20 books, including *William Faulkner; Lion in the Garden: Interviews with William Faulkner, 1926–1962;* and *Faulkner's Place*, from which this excerpt is taken.]

Quentin does, of course, drown in *The Sound and the Fury*, and his whole section could be, and has been, spoken of as just such a dying flashback. Interestingly, it is a flashback full of voices, of remembered conversation and speech, chiefly Mr. Compson's but also Caddy's and Shreve's and several others'. In *Absalom, Absalom!* Quentin is torn apart by the various conflicting voices juxtaposed within his memory, and it is possible to see in that novel the ultimate realization, what Faulkner himself might have called the apotheosis, of just the kind of retrospective, re-evaluating role that Quentin was originally invented to perform—though made much more complex, and much more somber, as a consequence of Faulkner's increased maturity both as man and as artist. One can even think of the entire novel, deliberately located by Faulkner just a few months before that suicide of which *The Sound and the Fury* has already informed us, as constituting Quentin's drowning flashback—and of those desperate concluding words about the South (*"I don't hate it! I don't hate it!"*) as embodying his final thoughts as he goes down for the last time. One *can* think this, although, as I shall argue later, I'm not at all sure that one should.

The irony in all this is that by the time *Absalom* was written and published, any such comprehensive structuring had long been shattered beyond repair, most obviously by Faulkner's having killed off Quentin in *The Sound and the Fury*—even though that did not prevent his occasionally re-using Quentin, unnamed, as a convenient narrative perspective: thus the unidentified narrator of "The Old People" (as published in *Harper's* for September 1940) is the same person to whom Sam Fathers told the story of "A Justice." But if that pattern was indeed conceived in retrospective terms— and *Sartoris* (*Flags in the Dust*) and the various stories narrated by Quentin all look back at the past from the vantage point of the narrative present—it was in any case doomed to eventual destruction by its failure to make allowance for the author's own existence in time, for the likelihood of his continuing to live and write on into the future, beyond the frozen moment, whenever it was originally intended to be, of Quentin's death. Backward and past obsessed though it might seem and be, even Yoknapatawpha, even northern Mississippi, could not remain motionless and unchanging. This was something Faulkner came to understand very clearly in later years, when the concept of life as motion became central to his thought and his work, and that understanding was no doubt sharpened and confirmed, within his own creative experience, by the way in which Yoknapatawpha itself had so rapidly and so radically burst the bonds of its initial time- and map-bound conception.

—Michael Millgate, *Faulkner's Place* (Athens, GA: University of Georgia Press, 1997): pp. 44–45

Plot Summary of
Absalom, Absalom!

Absalom, Absalom! opens in the office of Miss Rosa Coldfield soon after Quentin Compson has arrived. Miss Coldfield had summoned Quentin to her home to voice her version of the legendary tale of her "nothusband," Thomas Sutpen. Rosa is one of the many storytellers in this complex novel who offer as many versions of Thomas Sutpen's mysterious emergence and legacy in Jefferson, Mississippi. Rosa acknowledges that Quentin is going away to Harvard and suggests that if he were to become a writer, he could write a book on the complex story of Thomas Sutpen.

Faulkner's nonlinear, stream-of-consciousness narrative style is strongly in evidence in *Absalom, Absalom!,* which weaves the spoken voices of the storytellers and the internal ponderings of the listener—a role given almost exclusively to Quentin. Like most of the inhabitants of Jefferson, Quentin has grown up under the "cloud" of the Thomas Sutpen story. In a conversation he has with his father following the encounter in Miss Coldfield's home, Mr. Compson reveals that Quentin's grandfather was the closest approximation to a friend that Thomas Sutpen ever had in Jefferson, and that Rosa had likely summoned Quentin because of this connection. "So maybe she considers you partly responsible through heredity for what happened to her and her family through him," he tells his son.

The narrative returns to Rosa, who talks about Thomas Sutpen's arrival in Jefferson and of his need for a respectable woman, which he found in Rosa's sister Ellen, whom he eventually married. She also speaks of the two children they had, Henry and Judith, and the establishment of "Sutpen's Hundred," the land on which he established an estate some miles out of town. Rosa discusses his brutish nature and Ellen's subsequent transformation into a near recluse. She mentions Thomas's seemingly unwarranted objection to his daughter Judith's engagement to Charles Bon—an objection which the reader discovers later is at the heart of the Sutpen controversy—and she also speaks of her sister's untimely death. After her sister's death, Rosa says, she agreed to marry Thomas Sutpen, but the engagement was broken off not long after. The first chapter ends as Rosa tells of her sister's poorly attended wedding and their life on Sutpen's Hundred.

In **Chapter Two** Faulkner presents General Compson, Quentin's grandfather, who conveys his own insights about Thomas Sutpen to his son, Quentin's father. The reader learns that Thomas was known to keep company with what the town folk referred to as "wild Negroes." Sutpen spoke with these men in a language that many believed to be demonic—though it was actually a form of French that he picked up while seeking his fortune in the West Indies. With the help of these "wild" men, Thomas erected his mansion in the woods. General Compson discusses Sutpen's skill as an architect and the patience with which he went homeless for two years while it was being constructed—as did his workers.

Once he moved into his mansion, Sutpen became more social, inviting some of the townsmen out for card-playing, food, and drink. He established a plantation, where he harvested cotton from seeds that he, General Compson, had supplied. Sutpen's final step in establishing Sutpen's Hundred was to install the common furnishings of home and then go into town and find a wife. Instead of courting a woman with a sizable dowry, as many townspeople had expected him to do, Thomas Sutpen chose Ellen Coldfield, the daughter of a shopkeeper. When they marry, they send out a great number of invitations, but few actually attend the ceremony.

Chapter Three opens as Mr. Compson reveals that Clytemnestra (called Clytie), the daughter of one of Sutpen's black servants, was also Sutpen's daughter. He also reveals that at one time, the Coldfields visited "Sutpen's Hundred" almost every week, until Henry went off to college and Rosa became a young woman. The remainder of the chapter details the transition of Sutpen's Hundred. It begins when Thomas goes to New Orleans for reasons unknown to Ellen. During his absence, Henry (Ellen and Thomas's son) brings home a friend from college named Charles Bon. Henry's sister, Judith, becomes engaged to Charles, even though they scarcely know each other—a union that Thomas strenuously opposes. Soon after the engagement, however, Henry and Charles disappear, leaving Henry's birthright "voluntarily repudiated" and Judith's marriage to Charles uncertain. As the chapter ends, the reader learns that Ellen has died.

Mr. Compson adds some detail to the Sutpen story in **Chapter Four**. He tells Quentin about Henry's love for Charles Bon that leads him to forfeit his inheritance. It is also revealed that Charles is legally married to an black woman, and that they have a child in New

Orleans. This seems to explain Thomas' objection to the wedding of Charles and Judith, as well as to the reason behind Thomas' mysterious trips to New Orleans. Mr. Compson says that four years later, Henry kills Charles, and he describes this as a heroic act that saved his sister. As the reader is exposed to Mr. Compson's recreation of Henry's relationship with Charles Bon, it becomes apparent that Faulkner believes that the process of telling a story is as important as the story itself. It remains unclear whether Mr. Compson's version of the tale is true. Yet he shows his son a letter that Charles Bon wrote to Judith, in which he stated that their wedding plans had not changed.

The narrative shifts to Rosa Coldfield describing her residence at Sutpen's Hundred with Clytie and Judith after Charles Bon's death and Henry's departure. She accepts Thomas's offer of marriage, but he does not acknowledge her again until one day when he suggests that they marry only after she produces a male heir by him. Disgusted and angry, Rosa leaves Sutpen Hundred for her original home.

The events of the next two chapters take place in Quentin's dorm room at college, just after he receives a letter telling him that Rosa Coldfield has passed away. This letter sparks a conversation between Quentin and his roommate, Shreve, about the Sutpen story. Again, the reader is faced with another version of the same story, though in this section, the conversational narrative proves revealing. It seems that Rosa's father boarded himself in the attic and starved to death to avoid being drafted by the Confederate army. Quentin and Shreve also discuss Charles Bon's return to town with his legal wife and son. They speak about Sutpen's decision to go to the West Indies in an attempt to make his fortune, and how he had married and had a child there, ultimately leaving them behind as though they were material goods. The reader also discovers that Charles Bon is actually Thomas Sutpen's son, suggesting that Henry's motive for murdering Bon was not out of jealousy or to prevent bigamy, but to stop an incestuous relationship.

In the third-person perspective of the book's final chapters, the reader learns another possible motive for the murder of Charles Bon—fear of miscegenation. Thomas Sutpen tells his son that Charles's mother was not Spanish, as he had been led to believe, but part black. He makes it clear that because of this, Henry must prevent Charles from marrying Judith. The novel ends as Rosa and Quentin return to Sutpen's Hundred to investigate stories of a mysterious person who has been living there. The resident is Henry, who says he has returned there to die. ❈

List of Characters in
Absalom, Absalom!

Thomas Sutpen is the central character in the novel. His mysterious arrival in Jefferson and his subsequent rise to power becomes a local bit of folklore. Thomas constructs an estate called "Sutpen's Hundred" around which the majority of the novel's events center.

Quentin Compson is the primary figure in the complex narrative process, acting both as listener and storyteller. The reader learns many of the details of the Thomas Sutpen story while Quentin and his college roommate, Shreve, discuss the story in their dorm room.

Rosa Coldfield is the first character the reader encounters. She summons Quentin to her home not only to tell him the story of Thomas Sutpen but also to have him accompany her to the estate to investigate a mysterious resident.

Shreve McCannon is Quentin's roommate at Harvard.

Henry Sutpen, the son of Thomas Sutpen, kills Charles Bon, with whom he had an intimate relationship and to whom his sister, Judith, becomes engaged.

Charles Bon is the biracial son of Thomas Sutpen and a black Haitian woman. He is killed by Henry Sutpen after he becomes engaged to Judith.

Judith Sutpen is the daughter of Thomas Sutpen and Ellen Coldfield.

Ellen Coldfield, Rosa Coldfield's sister, is the wife of Thomas Sutpen. She dies at Sutpen's Hundred soon after Judith and Charles become engaged.

Clytemnestra Sutpen is the daughter of Thomas Sutpen by a Haitian servant of his. ❀

Critical Views on
Absalom, Absalom!

MICHAEL MILLGATE ON QUENTIN COMPSON'S
SOUTHERN IDENTITY

[Michael Millgate is a professor of English at the University
of Toronto, where he has taught since 1967. He has
authored or edited more than 20 books, including *William
Faulkner* and *Lion in the Garden: Interviews with William
Faulkner, 1926–1962*. Here, Millgate discusses Quentin
Compson as a repository of Southern history.]

Quentin's final failure to resolve the quasi-authorial problems
which confront him is closely related to his passivity, which itself
has important implications for his initial and much more suc-
cessful role of listener. It is the availability and apparent suitability
of Quentin as an audience which at once provokes and modifies
the recitals of Miss Rosa and Mr. Compson; the particular flavour
of their narrations is largely determined by their awareness of who
and what Quentin is. As a young, intelligent Southerner, eldest son
of his family and hence destined to become "the Compson," about
to leave the homeland for the foreign environment of New England and Harvard, Quentin seems an appropriate repository for a
story which they both dimly recognise as embodying some quin-
tessential and symbolic relationship to the whole Southern experience, and which they both hand on to Quentin as if it were some
dark inheritance from the Southern past. At the very beginning of
the novel there are already two Quentins:

> Then hearing would reconcile and he would seem to
> listen to two separate Quentins now—the Quentin
> Compson preparing for Harvard in the South, the deep
> South dead since 1865 and peopled with garrulous out-
> raged baffled ghosts, listening, having to listen, to one of
> the ghosts which had refused to lie still even longer than
> most had, telling him about ghost-times; and the
> Quentin Compson who was still too young to deserve yet
> to be a ghost, but nevertheless having to be one for all
> that, since he was born and bred in the deep South the
> same as she was—the two separate Quentins now talking

to one another in the long silence of notpeople, in not-
language, . . .

As the book proceeds, Quentin is buffeted to and fro not only
between these two facets of himself but between the conflicting alle-
giances to differing interpretations of Sutpen and his story which
seem to be demanded of him by Miss Rosa, by his father, and by the
information he is able to collect for himself from other sources. His
own version of the story contains, suspended in uneasy co-existence,
substantial elements of all these interpretations, each of which
attracts him for different reasons at different times. He never manages to free himself from these presences to the extent that would
permit a radical re-interpretation of the whole Sutpen story and its
Southern context, and he remains to the end that fatally divided and
ghost-dominated personality to whom we are introduced at the
beginning of the book:

> his very body was an empty hall echoing with sonorous
> defeated names; he was not a being, an entity, he was a
> commonwealth. He was a barracks filled with stubborn
> back-looking ghosts. . . .

—Michael Millgate, *The Achievement of William Faulkner* (Athens,
GA: University of Georgia Press, 1963): pp. 155–56

⊛

JOSEPH GOLD ON MORALITY IN *ABSALOM, ABSALOM!*

[Joseph Gold has taught English at the University of Mani-
toba, Winnipeg, and is the author of a number of articles on
American fiction. In this excerpt, Gold discusses the concept of morality among Faulkner's characters.]

The career of Sutpen in *Absalom, Absalom!* holds a fascination for
Quentin, the modern man in search of a moral tradition, only
because it provides a key to an understanding of a whole society
and its foundations. Like Flem Snopes in *The Town*, Sutpen
becomes accepted by society:

. . . he was accepted; he obviously had too much money now to be rejected or even seriously annoyed any more. He accomplished this—got his plantation to running smoothly (he had an overseer now; it was the son of that same sheriff who had arrested him at his bride-to-be's gate on the day of the betrothal) within ten years of the wedding, and now he acted his role too—a role of arrogant ease and leisure which, as the leisure and ease put flesh on him, became a little pompous.

He has measured up to the demands of his peers, and, ironically, they are forced to recognize and acknowledge their own parody. Sutpen's rise contains all the faults of the rise of the plantation system: the total absence of human considerations; the ruthless and yet pointless goal of material ease; a search for social dominance. William R. Poirier has particularly emphasized the inhuman character of Sutpen's rise. He tells us that Sutpen pursues his design "with a complete insensitivity to human character." But these faults are not newly found in Sutpen; they are part of what he copies.

> Yes, mad, yet not so mad. Because there is a practicality to viciousness: the thief, the liar, the murderer even, has faster rules than virtue ever has; why not madness too? If he was mad, it was only his compelling dream which was insane and not his methods.

Sutpen's dream is the dream of all his contemporaries.

Quentin's interest in the Sutpen story is the result of his confusion as to his own moral role in society. To understand one's past is to better understand oneself. Quentin's grandfather was Sutpen's best, indeed only, friend, and thus the tie between Quentin and Sutpen is made closer. There is no doubt that to understand Quentin's interest in his past, one needs to be more fully acquainted with his present as it is revealed in *The Sound and the Fury*. The chaos of the present, the realization of his moral inadequacy, leads Quentin to seek some reason in the tradition: "Within the chaotic nature of Sutpen's history and Rosa's 'demonizing,' Quentin tries to find some human value adhering to what is apparently a representative anecdote of his homeland." A look at the tradition does provide him with the terrible truth about his own place in time. Significantly enough, even

Shreve, the remote, intellectual Canadian, becomes involved in the story, for it is really his story too. For the young it is quite clear that their shaping spirit rests in the past; Bon and Henry must look to their father for the cause of their problems. The four young men of the novel have in common their understanding of their own help-lessness as victims of an amoral past, a past which irresponsibly dis-regarded the future effects of its actions and beliefs.

—Joseph Gold, *William Faulkner: A Study in Humanism From Metaphor to Discourse* (Norman, OK: University of Oklahoma Press, 1967): pp. 30–31

⊗

PANTHEA REID BROUGHTON ON OBJECTIFICATION IN FAULKNER'S NOVELS

[Panthea Reid Broughton is a professor of English at Louisiana State University. She has published reviews in *Saturday Review World, Chicago Sun Times,* and the *New York Times Book Review.* In this excerpt, Broughton dis-cusses Faulkner's use of characters as abstract symbols.]

In *Absalom, Absalom!* Ellen is not the only character who renders a human being an abstraction by valuing him according to his utility alone. She herself is, in fact, the subject and victim of just such a dehumanizing estimate. For, to her husband, Ellen is only the inherent embodiment, the mere shape of respectability. Sutpen had come "to town to find a wife exactly as he would have gone to the Memphis market to buy livestock or slaves." Ellen is chosen ratio-nally, ruthlessly, because she represents impeccable respectability. Sutpen values Ellen, the architect, his slaves (the two women among them chosen probably "with the same care and shrewdness with which he chose the other livestock" only for what he can get out of them. Like octoroons who are, according to Mr. Compson, "more valuable as commodities than white girls," these people are, to Sutpen, only so much merchandise. For, with Sutpen, as with the group commander in *A Fable,* man is not a "gallant and puny crea-ture" but a mere "functioning machine." Thus he has interest in Rosa

Coldfield only if she can produce a son for him; he *"spoke the bald outrageous words* ⟨propositioning Rosa⟩ *exactly as if he were consulting with Jones or with some other man about a bitch dog or a cow or mare."*

Throughout the fiction, disastrous consequences result from seeing human beings as abstract symbols, using them as means to an end. Treated as symbol of her mother's shame or of her uncle's lost job, Caddy Compson's daughter Quentin hardly has a chance to develop into a complete individual. She runs away from home and is not heard of again. Eula Varner Snopes commits suicide so that Flem will no longer be able to own and manipulate her like a piece of merchandise on a seller's market. In *Light in August,* Gail Hightower has considered the girl he married as little more than an abstract shape embodying the things he wants from her. As he himself comes to realize, "'You took her as a means toward your own selfishness. As an instrument to be called to Jefferson.'" Her flight, adultery, and suicide are reactions motivated by a simple and pathetic attempt to declare her human identity. Joe Christmas' violence toward himself and others may, similarly, be understood as a reaction against the various abstract identities that haunt him and against the relationship with his foster father who accepts the boy only after examining him with "the same stare with which he might have examined a horse or a secondhand plow."

In *Absalom, Absalom!* furthermore, it is because they have been treated as just so many usable objects that characters react so vehemently. In that novel, acts of violence are reactions to rejection; they are assertions of personal identity and individuality; they are protests which proclaim *I am not an object.* After his discovery that to the planters his people were mere cattle, Thomas Sutpen formulated the design which was simply a violent attempt to wrest from life an identity for himself. Rejected by him, Eulalia Bon has used her son as an agent of vengeance against Sutpen. (The vengeance theory is Quentin and Shreve's interpretation, but it seems to be validated by context and Faulkner's remark that Shreve's hypotheses are "probably true enough.") And certainly the rejected Rosa Coldfield does want to be "an instrument of retribution" against Sutpen. Rejected by his father, Bon too seeks vengeance; he is perhaps using the marriage plans as a lever to force recognition from Sutpen. But if Henry kills him, Bon will in turn deny his

Sutpen kin. That is probably why he exchanges Judith's picture for that of the octoroon mistress and child. If he lives, the pictures may be reversed again. But if he is killed and the locket opened, Bon wants to be identified with the octoroon mistress, not with the Sutpens who rejected him. Charles Etienne de Saint Velery Bon too, in his fights first with black men then with white men, is attempting through violence to find his identity. His marriage to the black, apelike woman is a final vengeful gesture to make concrete his abstract identity as a black.

—Panthea Reid Broughton, *William Faulkner: The Abstract and the Actual* (Baton Rouge: Louisiana State University Press, 1974): pp. 70–72

⊛

LINDA KAUFFMAN ON FEMALE ANGER IN *ABSALOM, ABSALOM!*

[Linda Kauffman was a Fellow at the National Humanities Center of the Research Triangle Park at Chapel Hill, NC. She has published articles and reviews in *Mississippi Quarterly, Nineteenth Century Fiction,* and *The Georgia Review.* In this excerpt, Kauffman discusses Rosa Coldfield as a symbol of unacceptable female anger.]

Lovers' discourses have striking similarities in mood and motif, tone and technique. Their abiding themes are love and hate, seduction and betrayal, desire and despair. They frequently combine elements of the classic tragic tirade with the intense subjectivity of the epistolary form or the monologue. Of all the narratives in *Absalom, Absalom!*, Rosa Coldfield's has the most personal immediacy and the most passionate intensity. Far more than Quentin, she is the one who is most actively engaged in her narrative. Yet she has been dismissed as a "frustrated spinster," as if those two words were simply redundant. Although Rosa has much in common with such grand obsessives as Dickens' Miss Havisham in *Great Expectations* and Mrs. Clennam in *Little Dorrit,* she is far more complex than the stereotypical jilted lover. This distorted perception of her is wholly shaped by Mr. Compson, Quentin, and Shreve, none of whom ever really sees Rosa as anything but a warped, bitter, outraged, pathetic old woman. Rosa is a text they all misread.

It is one thing to indulge in imaginative reconstructions of the long-dead Sutpen, Henry, Bon, and Judith. But Rosa is not remote—she is a living, breathing woman whose relations with Quentin and Mr. Compson are far more personal, immediate, and intimate. The Sutpens are ghosts; she is not. Yet both men try to make Rosa as well into a ghost. When Quentin asks his father why he must answer Rosa's summons, for instance, Mr. Compson replies, "Years ago we in the South made our women into ladies. Then the War came and made the ladies into ghosts. So what else can we do, being gentlemen, but listen to them being ghosts?" They try to distance themselves from her by thus reducing her complexity. But if they cannot even comprehend the living woman in front of them, what hope is there of comprehending the long-dead Sutpens? This is what Shreve implies when he confronts Quentin at the end by saying, "You dont even know about the old dame, the Aunt Rosa. . . . You dont even know about her." Rosa resists reduction, however, as Shreve senses when he reflects that "She refused at the last to be a ghost." She refuses to allow herself to be reduced to some stereotypical figure of mere pathos and fury.

Female fury, indeed, is one of the obsessions that pervades the consciousness of males in the novel. The reductive view of Rosa, moreover, may stem from a fundamental uneasiness among characters *in* the novel and critics *of* the novel with the idea of female fury. "The dread and fear of females," after all, is something men draw in "with the primary mammalian milk." The words here are Grandfather Compson's, but the idea reverberates throughout the novel. What is fascinating is that Faulkner juxtaposes the complex with the reductive view of female anger by creating not one but two outraged women in *Absalom, Absalom!* The second is Eulalia Bon, the Creole wife whom Sutpen abandons, who is wholly invented by Quentin and Shreve. The Gothic is actually more pervasive in their imaginations than in Rosa's, for Eulalia resembles another Creole from the West Indies who is probably the most famous figure of fury in fiction: Bertha Mason, Rochester's mad wife in *Jane Eyre*. Bertha's heritage is tainted by hereditary madness; Eulalia's is allegedly "tainted" by Negro blood.

—Linda Kauffman, "Devious Channels of Decorous Ordering: A Lover's Discourse in *Absalom, Absalom!*" *Modern Fiction Studies* 29, no. 2 (Summer 1983): pp. 186–87

[Walter Taylor is a professor of English at the University of Texas at El Paso. He has published articles on Faulkner in *Southern Review, American Literature, South Atlantic Quarterly,* and *Southern Humanities Review.* In this excerpt, Taylor discusses the emergence of Clytie's secret.]

Faulkner was saving the full revelation of Clytie's secret for his "protagonist": it remained for Quentin to guess the truth, so that he and Shreve were able to put together an even more complex Sutpen. Quentin's father, it appeared, had passed on, without understanding, certain facts about Sutphen that he had learned from General Compson. Sutpen's Hundred represented Sutpen's second, not his first, attempt to establish that "design." The first was in Haiti, and he seemed to have succeeded when he saved the lives of his employer and his family by putting down a black rebellion. In telling the story Sutpen made himself sound like a hero in a cosmic Manichaean struggle: he simply "went out and subdued them," he told General Compson. His reward was marriage to his employer's daughter. But his triumph would not be quite so simple. Calvin Burden, who thought his grandson had a "black dam" and a "black look," could have told Sutpen that the more one wrestled with the dark powers, the more they left their mark. Sutpen discovered this when his wife gave him a son. For the first time he became aware of a fact that would "have . . . voided and frustrated . . . the central motivation of his entire design": his wife had African blood. This was the reality that had driven Sutpen from Haiti to Mississippi, and it was this reality that Miss Rosa found Clytie sealing off from her at the foot of the stairs: Sutpen's Haitian son was Charles Bon, and his presence in Yoknapatawpha County meant, as it had in Haiti, that Sutpen's "design" would be "voided and frustrated."

As Sutpen struggled to explain his life to General Compson, the Manichaean quality of his innocence emerged. Sutpen had provided for the mother and child, he said; and he had resigned all rights to the property he had acquired with the marriage "in order that I might repair whatever injustice I might be considered to have done." Where had he gone wrong? "You see," he told Quentin's grandfather, "I had a design in mind"; but he could not see how he was responsible for anything else. "Whether it was a good or a bad design is beside the point; the question is, Where did I make the mistake in it⟨?⟩" What Sutpen could not see was that his "mistake" was his "design." Spawned in his shock at discovering a world in the Tidewater that seemed the antithesis of his mountain innocence, the "design" allowed him to see the world only in terms of that innocence. Cavaliers like General Compson had inherited a tradition of *noblesse oblige* that allowed them to accept the responsibility for their own and other people's mistakes; but Puritan Sutpen could not see that he owed the woman anything, and Quentin's grandfather could scarcely believe what he was hearing. "What kind of . . . purblind innocence," he wanted to know, "would have warranted you in the belief that you could have bought immunity from her for no other coin but justice?" Conceived in the Manichaean self-righteousness that allowed him to cast himself only as the exemplar of light, Sutpen's "design" assured its own destruction by the powers of darkness.

> —Walter Taylor, *Faulkner's Search for a South* (Chicago: University of Illinois Press, 1983): pp. 103–104

⟨♪⟩

Linda Wagner-Martin on Rosa Coldfield's Rage

[Linda Wagner-Martin has taught at Michigan State University and the University of North Carolina. Her writings include *"The Age of Innocence": A Novel of Ironic Nostalgia* and *Telling Women's Lives: The New Biography*. Here, Wagner-Martin discusses Rosa Coldfield's rage as expressed in her language.]

Faulkner's "text" of Rosa's narrative is dominated from the first by a view of her as daughter. She meets Quentin in "what Miss Coldfield still called the office because her father had called it that," her habits of language and behavior formed by that father-daughter relationship. The forty-three years that have passed since she assumed her black garb might mark either the death of Goodhue Coldfield in 1864 or Sutpen's insult in 1866; those years are emphasized because Faulkner's attention falls on her long-unexpressed story, her "grim haggard amazed" voice, her "impotent yet indomitable frustration" paralleling her "impotent and static rage." The "crucified child" as she is pictured—sitting in "the chair that was so tall for her that her legs hung straight and rigid as if she had iron shinbones and ankles, clear of the floor . . . like children's feet"—has remained a child because she has never expressed that static rage directed at both father and non-husband, family and world.

The language that Rosa uses reflects that rage. Rosa says "tore violently"; Quentin writes "built." Rosa says "without gentleness begot," and Quentin omits the first two words. Though she rages within this language, she also tries to confine her image of Sutpen to "a scene peaceful and decorous as a schoolprize water color." Her art attempts to transform, but it fails as Quentin heightens the romantic elements of Sutpen's life. (It is Quentin's romanticism the reader responds to, not Rosa's telling, in thinking Sutpen superior in any way.) Rosa's focus is on the family of Sutpen, himself, the two children, and "the mother, the dead sister Ellen: this Niobe without tears," the mother who sacrificed everything for the children who were slain; but Rosa insists on her own role in the configuration: "I, a child, a child, mind you." Keeping Quentin's attention on her role in this macabre family romance, represented by her imaginary photo of parents and children, "the conventional family group of the period," from which she is absent, Rosa builds her own narrative, her accumulation of bad fortune so that at twenty, "an orphan a woman and a pauper," she had to turn for existence to her only kin, the family of her sister. The peak of Rosa's anguish occurs in the long paragraph stressing the guilt of her father's role in giving Ellen to Sutpen, in allowing that family group to exist. Her use of refrain signals her intensity: "But that it should have been our father, mine and Ellen's father of all of them that he knew. . . . That it should have been our father." Her jeremiad calls the reader's attention to the repetition of "our father," the prayerful term that suggests Rosa's strained apostasy, the daughter's willed deification of the father who would do no wrong but did numerous wrongs, increasing to the final one, of abandonment through voluntary separation and death.

—Linda Wagner-Martin, "Rosa Coldfield as Daughter: Another of Faulkner's Lost Children." In *Studies in American Fiction* 19, no. 1 (Spring 1991): pp. 4–5

ROBERT DALE PARKER ON THE HISTORY BEHIND *ABSALOM, ABSALOM!*

[Robert Dale Parker teaches at the University of Illinois at Urbana-Champaign. He is the author of *Faulkner and the Novelistic Imagination* and *The Unbeliever: The Poetry of Elizabeth Bishop*. In this excerpt, Parker discusses the history of Faulkner's characters in *Absalom, Absalom!*]

In American culture at large, Faulkner found his growing anguish over race relations, which would culminate in his novels of the 1940s. In literature, Harriet Beecher Stowe's *Uncle Tom's Cabin* and Mark Twain's *Adventures of Huckleberry Finn* and *Pudd'nhead Wilson* helped set the literary and cultural atmosphere for thinking about race relations, along with other novels—whether Faulkner read them or not—such as George Washington Cable's *The Grandissimes,* James Weldon Johnson's *The Autobiography of an Ex-Colored Man,* or Nella Larsen's *Quicksand* and *Passing*. Most of these works, like some of Faulkner's novels, explore the topic of mixed racial ancestry.

Absalom, Absalom! addresses older literatures as well. Its title alludes to the Old Testament story of David and his son Absalom (2 Sam. 13–19.4). Its language suggests the grandeur of Shakespeare's *Hamlet, Lear,* and *Othello*. And the novel evokes the familial and even national doom that hangs over Aeschylus's *Oresteia,* as well as over Faulkner's own earlier novel, *The Sound and the Fury*.

Indeed, the history in *Absalom, Absalom!* also comes out of Faulkner's personal and professional history. It is his sixth novel set in his imaginary Yoknapatawpha county—the county he sketched for the famous map at the back—and it is partly a sequel to *The Sound and the Fury*. While no one needs to read *The Sound and the Fury* to read *Absalom, Absalom!*, each novel can influence how we read the other. Still, though the two novels are related, they do not depend on each other, so that I will refer to *The Sound and the Fury* fairly often, but not in a way that my larger argument depends on. *The Sound and the Fury* focuses on the Compson family and its decay, including Quentin Compson's despair when his unmarried sister Caddy turns sexually active. Quentin wants to keep Caddy from leaving him. Partly for that reason, when she gets pregnant he explains to their father that he and Caddy have committed incest, but his father knows that Quentin is lying. Then, in June 1910, at the end of his first year at Harvard, Quentin drowns himself. Neither Quentin's sister nor his suicide gets mentioned in *Absalom, Absalom!* But readers who know about these concerns from the earlier novel may hear them echoing in the later work.

—Robert Dale Parker, *Absalom, Absalom!: The Questioning of Fictions* (Boston: Twayne Publishers, 1991): pp. 8–9

℘

DEBORAH CLARKE ON FANTASTIC WOMEN AND NOT-MOTHERS IN *ABSALOM, ABSALOM!*

[Deborah Clarke is a professor of English and Women's Studies at Pennsylvania State University. She is the author of *Robbing the Mother: Women in Faulkner.* In this excerpt, Clarke addresses the significance of women within the novel.]

Women, familiar creatures with fantastic dimensions, exemplify Faulkner's oxymoronic world, a familiar world made strange. In *Absalom, Absalom!,* a novel where questions of power and authority are so central, the presence of the women—and the fantastic nature of the women—attacks the dominant thematic and structural premises on which the novel rests. The result is a book which denies the very groundwork of its own authority, fictionalizing the Law of the Father yet also displacing the mother, for literal mothers are curiously absent, replaced by aunts; Rosa, her aunt, Judith, and Clytie overshadow Ellen, Eulalia, the octoroon, and Milly Jones. Maternal power is eerily transformed into a far more pervasive force, reaching beyond mothers and, for the first time in Faulkner's work, beyond white women as well.

In this, his most powerful novel, Faulkner confronts not just the feminine challenge to white patriarchy, but the racial challenge as well. Thomas Sutpen's dynasty goes down in flames in part because he fails to recognize daughters or racially mixed sons as potential heirs to his domain. However, Faulkner's most striking departure from his other work emerges in his presentation of important, interesting, and powerful African American women. While the theoretical racial questions, as always in Faulkner, are restricted primarily to male discussion and male concerns, the presence of Clytie and, to a lesser extent, of Eulalia and the octoroon highlights the bodily presence of racial difference, a difference which challenges white men and white women. Clytie, protector and avenger, figuratively embodies the forces which defeat white southern patriarchy and literally sets in motion the final stage of the fall of the house of Sutpen.

As the above cast of characters reveals, women, black or white, mothers or not, play a highly significant role in the novel. It is not surprising that a vast array of studies on the women of *Absalom* has replaced an era of criticism which focused almost exclusively on Quentin Compson and Thomas Sutpen. Yet amid these many excellent essays, remarkably little has been said about the power of the mother—or, rather, the notmother—and her significance in a book haunted by ghostly and uncanny events. In fact, the lack of literal mothers may be the ghostliest and uncanniest concern of a novel in which obsession with the generation of family and anguish over individual autonomy hold such crucial positions. Quentin Compson may decide that he has too many fathers (his own, Shreve, and Thomas Sutpen) and Charles Bon that he has too few, but where are the mothers whose procreation creates the father?

—Deborah Clarke, *Robbing the Mother: Women in Faulkner* (Jackson, MS: University Press of Mississippi, 1994): pp. 126–27

Works by
William Faulkner

The Marble Faun. 1924.

Soldiers' Pay. 1926.

Sherwood Anderson and Other Famous Creoles (editor). 1926.

Mosquitoes. 1927.

Sartoris. 1929.

The Sound and the Fury. 1929.

As I Lay Dying. 1930.

Sanctuary. 1931.

These 13. 1931.

Idyll in the Desert. 1931.

Light in August. 1932.

Salmagundi. 1932.

This Earth. 1932.

Miss Zilphia Gant. 1932.

A Green Bough. 1933.

Doctor Martino and Other Stories. 1934.

Pylon. 1935.

Absalom, Absalom! 1936.

The Unvanquished. 1938.

The Wild Palms. 1939.

The Hamlet. 1940.

Go Down, Moses and Other Stories. 1942.

A Rose for Emily and Other Stories. 1945.

The Portable Faulkner. Ed. Malcolm Cowley. 1946.

Intruder in the Dust. 1948.

Knight's Gambit. 1949.

Collected Stories. 1950.

Notes on a Horsethief. 1951.

Speech of Acceptance upon the Award of the Nobel Prize for Literature. 1951.

Requiem for a Nun. 1951.

Mirrors of Chartre Street. 1953.

The Faulkner Reader. 1954.

A Fable. 1954.

Big Woods. 1955.

Jealousy and Episode: Two Stories. 1955.

New Orleans Sketches. Ed. Ichiro Nishizaki. 1955.

The Segregation Decisions (with Benjamin E. Mays and Cecil Sims). 1956.

Faulkner at Nagano. Ed. Robert A. Jelliffe. 1956.

The Town. 1957.

New Orleans Sketches. Ed. Carvel Collins. 1958.

Three Famous Novels. 1958.

The Mansion. 1959.

The Reivers. 1962.

Selected Short Stories. 1962.

Early Prose and Poetry. Ed. Carvel Collins. 1962.

The Faulkner-Cowley File: Letters and Memories 1944–1962 (with Malcolm Cowley). 1966.

Essays, Speeches and Public Letters. Ed. James B. Meriwether. 1966.

The Wishing Tree. 1967.

Flags in the Dust. Ed. Douglas Day. 1973.

Selected Letters. Ed. Joseph Blotner. 1977.

Mayday. 1977.

Uncollected Stories. Ed. Joseph Blotner. 1977.

Helen: A Courtship and Mississippi Poems. 1981.

Faulkner's MGM Screenplays. Ed. Bruce F. Kawin. 1982.

Elmer. Ed. Dianne L. Cox. 1984.

Country Lawyer and Other Stories for the Screen. 1987.

Stallion Road: A Screenplay (with Louis D. Brodsky and Robert W. Hamblin). 1989.

Works about
William Faulkner

Abbott, Shirley. *Womenfolk: Growing Up Down South.* New York: Ticknor & Fields, 1983.

Barnett, Louise K. "The Speech Community of *The Hamlet.*" *Centennial Review 30* (Summer 1986): pp. 400–414.

Blotner, Joseph Leo. *Faulkner: A Biography.* New York: Random House, 1974.

Butler, Judith. *Gender Trouble: Feminism and the Subversion of Identity.* New York: Routledge, 1990.

Coleman, Rosemary. "Family Ties: Generating Narratives in *Absalom, Absalom!*" *Mississippi Quarterly* 41 (Summer 1988): pp. 19–32.

Davis, Thadious M. *Faulkner's "Negro": Art and the Southern Context.* Baton Rouge: Louisiana State University Press, 1983.

Dixon, Thomas, Jr. *The Clansman.* New York: Doubleday, Page and Co., 1905.

Duvall, John N. *Faulkner's Marginal Couple: Invisible, Outlaw, and Unspeakable Communities.* Austin: University of Texas Press, 1990.

Early, James. *The Making of "Go Down Moses."* Dallas: Southern Methodist University Press, 1972.

Fant, Joseph L., and Robert Ashley, eds. *Faulkner at West Point.* New York: Random House, 1964.

Fielder, Leslie. *Love and Death in the American Novel.* New York: Criterion Books, 1960.

Gwynn, Frederick L., and Joseph Blotner, eds. *Faulkner in the University.* Charlottesville: University of Virginia Press, 1959.

Howe, Irving. *William Faulkner: A Critical Study.* New York: Vintage Books, 1962.

Irwin, John. *Doubling and Incest/Repetition and Revenge: A Speculative Reading of Faulkner.* Baltimore: Johns Hopkins University Press, 1975.

Jacobus, Mary. *Reading Women: Essays in Feminist Criticism.* Ithaca: Cornell University Press, 1985.

Jehlen, Myra. *Class and Character in Faulkner's South.* New York: Columbia University Press, 1976.

Kerr, Elizabeth M. *William Faulkner's Gothic Domain.* Port Washington, NY: Kennikat Press, 1979.

Kinney, Arthur F. *Faulkner's Narrative Poetics: Style as Vision.* Amherst: University of Massachusetts Press, 1978.

Kirwan, Albert D. *Revolt of the Rednecks.* Lexington: University of Kentucky Press, 1951.

Levins, Lynn Gartrell. *Faulkner's Heroic Design: The Yoknapatawpha Novels.* Athens: University of Georgia Press, 1976.

Matthews, John T. *The Play of Faulkner's Language.* Ithaca: Cornell University Press, 1982.

Mortimer, Gail. *Faulkner's Rhetoric of Loss.* Austin: University of Texas Press, 1983.

O'Donnell, Patrick. "Sub Rosa: Voice, Body, and History in *Absalom, Absalom!*" *College Literature* 16 (1989): pp. 28–47.

Page, Sally R. *Faulkner's Women: Characterization and Meaning.* DeLand: Everett/Edwards, 1972.

Peters, Erskine Alvin. *The Yoknapatawpha World and Black Being.* Ann Arbor: University Microfilms International, 1976.

Schliefer, Ronald. "Faulkner's Storied Novel: 'Go Down Moses' and the Translation of Time." *Modern Fiction Studies* 28 (Spring 1982): pp. 109–27.

Schmitter, Dean Morgan, ed. *William Faulkner: A Collection of Criticism.* New York: McGraw Hill, 1973.

Sensibar, Judith L. *The Origins of Faulkner's Art.* Austin: University of Texas Press, 1984.

Slatoff, Walter J. *Quest for Failure: A Study of William Faulkner.* Westport, CT: Greenwood Press, 1972.

Spenko, James Leo. "The Death of Joe Christmas and the Power of Words," *Twentieth Century Literature* 28 (Fall 1982): pp. 252–68.

Sundquist, Eric J. *Faulkner: The House Divided.* Baltimore, Johns Hopkins University, 1983.

Wagner, Linda Welshimer, ed. *Four Decades of Faulkner Criticism.* East Lansing: Michigan State University Press, 1973.

Warren, Robert Penn, ed. *Faulkner: A Collection of Critical Essays.* Englewood Cliffs, NJ: Prentice Hall, 1966.

Wasson, Ben. *Count No 'Count.* Jackson: University Press of Mississippi, 1983.

Williams, David L. *Faulkner's Women: The Myth and the Muse.* Montreal: McGill-Queen's University Press, 1977.

Wyatt, David. *Prodigal Sons: A Study in Authorship and Authority.* Baltimore: Johns Hopkins University Press, 1980.

Index of
Themes and Ideas